CHARACTERISTICS OF THE SONS OF THE SUPERNATURAL

By
Dr Alidi J. Mpateya

Copyright

First Edition 2017

Ordering Information:
Quantity sales. Special discounts are available on quantity purchases by corporations, associations, and others. For details, contact us.

CONTACT DETAILS

TELEPHONE: (+27) 41 484 1687
MOBILE: (+27) 73 184 7996
Email: balidijm@gmail.com

DEDICATION

This book is dedicated to all the saints that are hungry for the supernatural move of God, who represent the present day truth. It is my prayer that it can be used as a resource for the advancement of the kingdom. And to my wife Katherine and my spiritual sons and daughters namely Tshenolo Mokonyama, Sibabalo Mbatsha, Lukhanyo M Kopsani and those who kept me in their prayers during the time of the birthing of this manuscript. And my beloved brother from another mother Simon Peter M.

FOREWORD

I have known Apostle Alidi for many years. I have seen this man of God move against the odds to accomplish what I have seen very few men do. He has a great vision to go back on television ministry and radio ministry so that he continues impacting men and women in the five continents of the world and beyond.

He is a father to many sons across the world. He makes us as Africans proud. His inspiration by the Holy Spirit to enter the world of putting pen to paper as it were is significant in the day and age we are living in. This work is a needed work to bring to this generation the need to revisit the fundamental aspects of our Christian walk with Christ.

We are living in a world where faith is substituted with logic, true worship is substituted with entertainment, deliverance is substituted with good counselling, psychology and the list can go on and on. Apostle Alidi addresses the fundamental truths of characteristics that define sons who walk in the supernatural power of the Holy Spirit.

God is a miracle working God. It is natural for God to do miracles. We as men and women who call God Father, should move in the supernatural power of the Holy Spirit. In his book The Characteristics of the Sons of the Supernatural, Apostle Alidi journeys with us through all the different facets of the supernatural character we need to experience.

He somehow artistically sketches the revelations that addresses supernatural prayer, supernatural deliverance, supernatural warfare, supernatural giving, that you can and will encounter in the life of sons and daughters who believe in being carriers of the supernatural power of the Holy Spirit. This book puts the Spirit of Glory back onto the centre stage. His focus on the Scriptures causes you to expose yourself to the mind of God on the subject he brings to you.
I trust that as you read this book you will be activated to grow in the Characteristics of Supernatural Sons!

Apostle Neville Goldman,
Ebenezer International, Port Elizabeth, South Africa
www.ebenezerinternational.org

ENDORSEMENT

THE CHARACTERISTICS OF THE SONS OF THE SUPERNATURAL

Characteristics of the Sons of the Supernatural is not only the title of this book. It also applies to the example that I see in my spiritual son, Alidi Mpateya of South Africa. When you read his book, you will gain new insight on what it takes to hear from God, preach what you hear, experience God's supernatural power, and yet stay on the pathway of humility.
This book concludes with an example from the beginning of Alidi's Christian life. When he first awakened to personal faith in Jesus Christ, almost immediately he heard God speak to him and he made an important decision to obey God's voice. He asked his pastor if he could preach in the church, and his discerning pastor said yes. As a result, he writes, after his first message, "That very night, one man stood up and made a public confession that through my preaching he was now going to obey God, as he had been resisting the calling of God in his life."

Faith, obedience, and preaching are vital factors in experiencing the supernatural power. So is the principle of humility. Pastor Alidi Mpateya reminds us that Jesus left us an example of humility that all Christians must recognize and follow. He writes, "For God to become a man is a picture of humility. It denotes the supernatural. It's unnatural for God to be a man. Jesus appeared irrelevant, but He was relevant all the time; he looked like He was backward and outdated. Why would God become a man? But through all that He did, He was ahead all the time; God works in reverse." "God works in reverse," he says. As the Scripture says in Isaiah 55:8, God's ways are not our ways. Pastor Alidi asks us to consider Moses' rise to power. He became a world leader known for great humility but earlier in life he had been "known for going where he wanted to go, executing what he wanted to execute," but he was changed by a supernatural encounter with God. "He was now a graduate of his past mistakes, and he came to acknowledge his total reliance on God through humility."

In our day, we live in a disturbed environment of angry confrontation and revenge. Our response should be an opposite spirit. Contrary to the spirit of revenge, he writes, "Humility does not respond to confrontation in the same spirit, rather it seeks to give in so that amicable resolves can be obtained. It takes the broken spirit of someone who does not believe in strife, [but] rather operates in humility to achieve unity and peace." He quotes Psalm 51:17, "The sacrifices of God are a broken spirit: a broken and a contrite heart, O God, thou wilt not despise."

If you are a Christian seeking more of the supernatural, you will find it here in an unexpected way. You will be led on this pathway by a man of God whose ministry is characterized by miracles, signs, and wonders, but you must read carefully. Commit yourself to live more fully by faith, constantly meditating on God's Word, and obey God in sacrificial humility. Then you will begin to understand at a deeper level what God wants you

to do so that He can trust you with His power.
Bishop Wellington Boone
Bishop Wellington Boone is a Black American evangelical Christian leader who was ranked by researcher George Barna and co-author Harry Jackson, Jr., as the number one Black American leader in racial reconciliation of the 20th Century. The Founder and chief prelate of the Fellowship of International Churches and church planter, author and public speaker.

TABLE OF CONTENTS

INTRODUCTION

In this book, I have expounded the topic of the Supernatural to the best of my ability. You will find that throughout the book, I have emphasized that all the sons of God have a new natural, the supernatural. The born-again experience enables believers to receive the DNA of the Spirit of God thus becoming partakers of God's divine nature. This supernatural nature is imparted to them from the moment they believe. Faith is supernatural, and Jesus is the beginning and the end of our faith. From the moment we receive Him as the Lord and Saviour of our lives, our journey of the supernatural begins. The natural man never understands the things of God. One has to be in the spirit to understand spiritual things, so they can only be understood in the realm of the Spirit.

But the natural [unbelieving] man does not accept the things [the teachings and revelations] of the Spirit of God, for they are foolishness [absurd and illogical] to him; and he is incapable of understanding them, because they are spiritually discerned and appreciated, [and he is unqualified to judge spiritual matters]. (1 Corinthians 2:14 AMP)

When one receives the supernatural DNA as a believer he is then given the grace to be able to follow Jesus the Christ. This submission and obedience is key to God's power being manifested. Thus, the believers become demonstrations and demonstrators of the Kingdom of God on earth. That enables them to engage in spiritual warfare that is fought in the spiritual realm,and are empowered to move in spiritual realms where angels move, and demons fight. As those born of a divine nature, they can effectively oppose satanic powers. The believer, due to his or her divine nature, can give to God the worship He seeks.

This is not based on what denominational affiliations they come from, rather it is found in their new supernatural relationship with God. As born- again men and women, they have a spiritual nature that interacts with God. At the same time, they have within this nature the grace of humility. Without humility, there is no real walk with God. He resists the proud.

This humility easily manifests due to the essential nature of the divine in the believer. In this position of humility, the believer has access to the power of the Holy Spirit to guide them in prayer. Their prayers are led by the Spirit, birthed by the Spirit and answered by the Spirit of God. Likewise, the believer receives the divine nature which affects their generosity. God is an abundant and giving God. Those with His divine nature are inspired and equipped to give generously to God and His ministry on the earth. The believer is to be God's mouth speaking in the Spirit on the earth. The Holy Spirit enables these believers to speak of God with clarity and authority.

The book successfully covers the subject of the supernatural characteristics of a believer that I have presented in a wide dimension of reality in ten chapters to help the believer understand what his/her role is in his/her walk of faith. As you go through this book I trust that you will have encounters that will enhance your walk of faith to go to the next level and cause su- pernatural activities to be realized.

CHAPTER I

THE SUPERNATURAL AND THE HOLY SPIRIT

The birth of Jesus Christ was announced through a supernatural encounter where God sent an angel to appear before His mother. This encounter was the pacesetter of the events that unfolded thereafter few things which transpired that day, the announcement of a child to be born by a woman who was going to conceive by the Holy Spirit. This had never happened anywhere, it was unheard of, it was going to take the Holy Spirit to perform the supernatural miracle of a child that was to be born.

A diagnostics of the events that took place before Jesus was born and how it relates to the supernatural According to the gospel accounts relating to the birth of Jesus, it all began with the visitation of an angel to His mother Mary. The announcement of the angel was emphasized that whatever was going to take place would be carried out by the Holy Spirit coming upon her. There is no God's supernatural outside of the working of the Holy Spirit, God's supernatural and the Holy Spirit are one and the same thing. You cannot have one and not have the other.

To a virgin espoused to a man whose name was Joseph, of the house of David; and the virgin's name was Mary. And the angel came in unto her, and said, Hail, thou that art highly favoured, the Lord is with thee: blessed art thou among women. And when she saw him, she was troubled at his saying, and cast in her mind what manner of salutation this should be. And the angel said unto her, Fear not, Mary: for thou hast found favour with God. And, behold, thou shalt conceive in thy womb, and bring forth a son, and shalt call his name JESUS. He shall be great, and shall be called the Son of the Highest: and the Lord God shall give unto him the throne of his father David: And he shall reign over the house of Jacob for ever; and of his kingdom there shall be no end. (Luke 1:27-33)

REASONING OF NATURAL VERSUS SUPERNATURAL

The supernatural encounter has a tendency of causing the natural man or his natural reasoning to be astonished. The supernatural is nothing but a wonder and a sign that can cause one to be afraid because it's not a day-to-day occurrence; hence Mary was overwhelmed by the news. However the angel assured her that what was going to happen to her was more than a blessing to her and to the entire world. Even after that brief explanation, she still wanted a further explanation. She then continued to engage the angel by seeking more clarity in the following passage:

Then said Mary unto the angel, How shall this be, seeing I know not a man? And the angel answered and said unto her, The Holy Ghost shall come upon thee, and the power of the Highest shall overshadow thee:

therefore also that holy thing which shall be born of thee shall be called the Son of God. (Luke 1:34-35)

She responded to the angel according to her natural reasoning; if she was going to have a child, how could that be? Since she was not yet married, but only engaged at that juncture. This serves as evidence that our Lord Jesus was born out of a supernatural occurrence.

Common sense and natural reasoning will seek clarification for such matters, under these circumstances. We must be reminded that this was a young woman who was engaged and not yet married. She did not know any man. It takes a man and a woman coming together intimately in order for a child to be born, hence the question from her "How can this be since I know not a man?" This was a valid scientific question on her part, however, the angel did not respond with a biological lecture, but rather with a supernatural response.
Angels are spirit beings and for them to appear to natural beings is a supernatural occurrence, so it was in this setting that the angel announced to her the answer was a supernatural one.

As we read in the above mentioned scripture, the angel's continual explanation was the process that was going to transpire and cause the miracle of that childbirth, which was a supernatural one. The angel responded and said it was going to take the Holy Spirit's involvement and activation for that supernatural activity to be established.

THE HOLY GHOST AT WORK IN ALL SUPERNATURAL ACTIVITIES

In most cases throughout the Word of God whenever a miracle took place it was by the working and involvement of the Holy Spirit. The Holy Spirit is the hand of God that establishes what God wants to be done here on the earth. He was mentioned in the account of creation; He is always mentioned where God does supernatural works. The Holy Spirit is part of the Godhead and He brings about supernatural activities. There is no supernatural activity without the Holy Ghost. The child that was to be born was created by the Holy Spirit's involvement.

The true supernatural activity is the direct result of the presence of the Holy Spirit, therefore Jesus came into this world supernaturally. The Bible says "he was anointed with the Holy Spirit and power."

How God anointed Jesus of Nazareth with the Holy Ghost and with power: who went about doing good, and healing all that were oppressed of the devil; for God was with him. (Acts 10:38)

The Holy Spirit always will always be associated with the power of God; you never hear the mention of the Holy Spirit without seeing the demonstration of the power of God. The above scripture alludes to the fact that Jesus was anointed with the Holy Spirit and power, and as a result he went about healing the sick, casting out devils and doing all good things. It takes the power of the Holy Spirit for good activities to be seen and for the demonstration of the power of God.

Jesus in His response to some Pharisees after a demonstration of His power pointed this out to them in the scripture below:

But if I with the finger of God cast out devils, no doubt the kingdom of God is come upon you. (Luke 11:20)

In the kingdom of God, the Holy Ghost is the one that God releases, in order to display that, where the Kingdom of God is, there is power. The kingdom is not in word, but is in power. The word power comes out of the Greek word 'Dunamis' which means dynamite. It also means authority from the word 'Exousia'. The word 'power' therefore means dynamite which speaks of power versus 'Exousia', which means authority. However, the Holy Spirit has both dynamite, and authority. For example Satan has power, but does not have authority. Authority means the right to use the power. One can have power, but not have the right to use it. Satan has power, but is not authorized to use it. The Holy Spirit has power and authority at the same time.

We can now come to understand how Jesus through the power of the Holy Spirit was able to accomplish good. In the kingdom of God it is absolutely impossible for one to do anything outside the power of the Holy Spirit. He raised the dead; He healed the sick by the power of the Holy Spirit at work in His life. There is no working of miracles outside the Holy Spirit. Jesus was born of the Holy Spirit, by the Holy Spirit, supernaturally. His mission, or assignment, was to raise a supernatural generation, a generation that would operate under the unction of the Holy Spirit just as He did, going about doing good, healing the sick, casting out devils and raising the dead, by the power of the Holy Ghost.

There is a popular story involving Nicodemus and Jesus. In this story Nicodemus goes to Jesus and asks Him questions pertaining to the Kingdom of heaven.
His question was as follows; "What must I do to enter the kingdom of God?". Jesus responded "You must be born-again".

Jesus answered and said unto him, Verily, verily, I say unto thee, Except a man be born again, he cannot see the kingdom of God.. Nicodemus parried, "Must I go back to my mother's womb?" Nicodemus saith unto him, How can a man be born when he is old? Can he enter the second time into his mother's womb, and be born? And Jesus said to him "that which is born of the Spirit is spirit and which is born of the flesh is flesh.
(John 3:3-6)

Jesus referred Nicodemus to a spiritual birth. Jesus came to introduce a supernatural generation, supernatural begets supernatural. Jesus was born through the Holy Ghost; the angel told Mary "that, which shall be born shall be called holy and shall be called the son of the living God."

He shall be great, and shall be called the Son of the Highest: and the Lord God shall give unto him the throne of his father David: (Luke 1:32)

To inherit the kingdom of God one must become a child of God, there is no spiritual activity outside the rebirth, and Jesus informed Nicodemus that he had to be born of the Spirit.

It is important to note the angel that visited Mary to announce the birth of Jesus the Christ began by visiting Zechariah the husband of Elizabeth. The angel announced to him that his wife was going to give birth to John, and the child's mission was to be the forerunner of Jesus, the Christ. The message was clear that John would be filled with the Holy Spirit from his mother's womb, and he was to move and function under the spirit of Elijah. He was going to be one of the greatest prophet who ever lived.
There is no greatness without the Holy Spirit. There are similar statements found in the announcement of the angel in both incidents. The angel specified that John was going to be great and he was going to be full of the Holy Ghost from his mother's womb as seen in the scripture below:

For he shall be great in the sight of the Lord, and shall drink neither wine nor strong drink; and he shall be filled with the Holy Ghost, even from his mother's womb. (Luke 1:15)

The angel said, because he was going to be filled by the Holy Spirit from his mother's womb all that he was to accomplish was going to be great. Jesus confirmed this in His own words saying, "there is no one greater than John among those born of women."

For I say unto you, among those that are born of women there is not a greater prophet than John the Baptist: but he that is least in the kingdom of God is greater than he. (Luke 7:28)

The reason being, the birth of John was unique, his assignment was to be the forerunner of Jesus, and as I alluded, he was to be filled with the Holy Spirit from his mother's womb. Please note that the greatness of John is again connected to the activity of the Holy Spirit. The sum of John the Baptist's ministry was due to the Holy Spirit's major role. His preaching and prophesying was great because of the Holy Ghost, hence those who are "born again" in the kingdom of God receive the Holy Spirit in power. This enables them to walk and work in the supernatural. Allow me to say they are sons of the supernatural. They exhibit and demonstrate, they are the movers and shakers under the function and unction of the power of the Holy Ghost.

Let us look at this account from the book according to Saint John. In the first chapter he points out to those who became believers that as many as believed in Him were given power or are included to become sons of God. This had nothing to do with the natural birth. It refers to the spiritual birth, that takes place through one's faith in Jesus the Christ; hence this statement, "as many as believed in Him were given the power to become sons of God" and part of the spiritual family. That means they were transformed from natural to supernatural beings. Their new natural becomes supernatural; at this point they can navigate in the spiritual realm in the way described in the scripture below:

But as many as received him, to them he gave power to become the sons of God, even to them that believe on his name: (John 1:12)

The above scripture speaks of people who have received the Holy Spirit because they have become believers, they have received the power, and the authority, to become sons of God.
They move in God, and God moves through them. It will be correct to say Jesus was born supernatural, to raise a supernatural generation that will move in the supernatural. John, the apostle, addressed an interesting subject when he used the words "those who believe in Him are given power to become sons of God." It is obvious he was addressing the spiritual birth as I mentioned earlier on. At this point we might want to bring in the account of Peter, the apostle, when he preached for the first time in the New Testament setting. This was just after being filled with the Holy Spirit together with the fellow disciples of Jesus. In Acts chapter two, we see the event that took place in what was referred to as the upper room. It was here when he preached and many were convicted by his preaching.

They wanted to know what to do next. Part of what the Holy Spirit does is to convict people of their sins, so that they can become children of God. Every time a supernatural encounter occurs it overwhelms the natural man. We have seen that in the angelic visitations to Zechariah and Mary; both of them were overwhelmed. The scripture in the book of Corinthians says the natural man does not receive spiritual things for they are foolishness unto him. On the occasion of Peter's preaching we find a similar response, where people begun to ask what to do next. Peter answered them as follows:

Then Peter said unto them, Repent, and be baptized every one of you in the name of Jesus Christ for the remission of sins, and ye shall re- ceive the gift of the Holy Ghost. For the promise is unto you, and to your children, and to all that are afar off, even as many as the Lord our God shall call. (Acts 2:38-39)

He invited them to a new life, which they would obtain by way of repentance. He pointed out to them that their sins will be forgiven, and they will also receive the baptism of the Holy Spirit. It was something that was unheard of. When he said that the Holy Ghost was available to them, he was preaching something that was totally new to the ears of his audience. Up to this point in the history of God's dealing with man, the Holy Spirit was only seen among the chosen few; it was exclusive, not inclusive. Peter was in agreement with the preaching of John the Baptist when he mentioned many who would believe and receive power.

I indeed baptize you with water unto repentance: but he that cometh after me is mightier than I, whose shoes I am not worthy to bear: he shall baptize you with the Holy Ghost, and with fire (Matthew 3:11)

John the Baptist had preached pointing to the fact that Jesus the Christ was the baptiser with the Holy Spirit and power. Peter was not only in agreement with John's preaching, he was also in agreement with the Old Testament prophet Joel. The prophet Joel alluded to the coming day when God would pour out his Spirit upon all mankind. Peter and John both endorsed this. According to Peter the supernatural begins at conversion.

He said you must repent, and he went on to say that those who repented would receive the Holy Spirit. He pointed out the promise was to them and their children and as many as God calls. The Holy Ghost is available to all believers, there is a misconception in some religious sectors that seeks to argue that just a few are eligible to receive the Holy Spirit. However, from the day of John the Baptist things changed. John was filled with the Holy Spirit from his mother's womb, and as part of his preaching he announced that Jesus was going to baptise with the Holy Spirit and power. Jesus brought an upgrade, which took all who believed him to new frontiers.

They were taken to new levels, and would navigate under the power of the Holy Ghost at the day of Pentecost. All of this was evident when the hundred and twenty persons gathered in the upper room were filled with the power of the Holy Spirit, and spoke in new tongues as the Spirit gave them utterance. This was a beginning of a new era; an era of the sons of the supernatural. All this was in agreement with the preaching of Jesus the Christ when He said:

But ye shall receive power, after that the Holy Ghost is come upon you: and ye shall be witnesses unto me both in Jerusalem, and in all Judaea, and in Samaria, and unto the uttermost part of the earth. When the Holy Ghost shall fall upon you and you shall be witnesses unto me and he also said the following He said to them greater works shall ye do than these. (Acts 1:8)

Jesus also said these words:

Verily, verily, I say unto you, He that believeth on me, the works that I do shall he do also; and greater works than these shall he do; because I go unto my Father (John 14:12)

He came to activate and commission a generation that will cast out devils, raise the dead and heal the sick. Jesus operated in the supernatural from at an early age as seen in the Scriptures; He taught in the synagogue and turned water into wine. His church has a supernatural DNA. Jesus spoke with the theologians of His day and they were amazed by His knowledge and His understanding.

And it came to pass, that after three days they found him in the temple, sitting in the midst of the doctors, both hearing them, and asking them questions. And all that heard him were astonished at his understanding and answers. And when they saw him, they were amazed: and his mother said unto him, Son, why hast thou thus dealt with us? Behold, thy father and I have sought thee sorrowing. (Luke 2:46-48)

Jesus turned water into wine supernaturally.

When the ruler of the feast had tasted the water that was made wine, and knew not whence it was: (but the servants who drew the water knew; the governor of the feast called the bridegroom, (John 2:9)

Peter, the apostle, mentioned that those who are in Christ have become a royal priesthood. This means Jesus came to establish a priesthood of all believers, who will have access to God, without going through a mediator. The Old Testament ordered believers to approach God through priests. The New Testament allows believers, who are filled with the Holy Spirit, to have access to the throne of grace and to commune with God. They worship him being led by the Holy Spirit that indwells them. This supernatural community, regardless of their age, race, or culture is marked by the Holy Spirit, and can do all the work of God through the unction of the Holy Spirit.

REFLECTIONS AND PRAYER ACTIVATION

1. Under what circumstances did the birth of Jesus occur? Supernatural _______________ where God sent an angel to appear before before his _______________.

2. What did the announcement of the angel emphasize? The announcement of the angel was emphasized that whatever was going to take place would be carried out by the __________________.

3. What was Mary's reply to the angel? Then said Mary unto the angel, How shall this be, seeing ____________________.

4. What did God anoint Jesus of Nazareth with? How God anointed Jesus of Nazareth with the _____________ and with ____________ : who went about doing good, and healing all that were oppressed of the devil; for God was with him.

5. How did Jesus cast out devils? But if I with the __________ cast out devils, no doubt the _______________of God is come upon you.

6. What must I do to enter the kingdom of God? Jesus answered and said unto him, Verily, verily, I say unto thee, Except a man be ____________, he cannot see the kingdom of God.

7. What happens when the Holy Spirit comes upon you? But ye shall receive ______________, after that the Holy Ghost is come upon you: and ye shall be ______________ unto me both in Jerusalem, and in all Judaea, and in Sa-

maria, and unto the ___________ of the earth. When the ______________ shall fall upon you and you shall be witnesses unto me and he also said the following He said to them greater works shall ye do than these.

1. Luke 1:34 [KJV]
2. Acts 10:38 [KJV]
3. Luke 11:20 [KJV]
4. John 3:3 [KJV]
5. Acts 1:8 [KJV]

PRAYER

God grant me the grace to have supernatural encounters with you through your Holy Spirit may I give birth to supernatural activities. May I not use my reasoning or wonder on how it is going to happen, may I trust you and your Holy Spirit to teach me all things. May I take heed to announcements that comes by your angels, open my eyes to see beyond my limitations. May I be in agreement with
your angels and messengers and fill me with the Holy Spirit and power that I may go about doing good things. Make me a global witness by your Holy Ghost in Jesus name amen.

CHAPTER 2

THE SUPERNATURAL DNA OF FOLLOWING

The story of Caleb is a very unique and interesting one it is important to note that all his achievements and his success where tied down to the fact he had such a high level of following. Because of the following reasons he demonstrated a following attitude to his leader in spite of his tribal background. He was so committed to serve that he rose up in the ranks and became one of the greatest leaders that even God bestowed upon him blessings and honour. A non-Hebrew among Hebrews who had such a heart of following that eventually gave him a reference that today his name is mentioned in the Holy Scriptures. His story is similar to the one of Ruth, also a non-Hebrew person whose heart was attached to her mother in-law that she refused to remain behind but followed her until she rose up the ranks and became the great grandmother of our Lord Jesus the Christ through her marriage to Boaz.

And she said, Behold, thy sister in law is gone back unto her people, and unto her gods: return thou after thy sister in law. And Ruth said, Entreat me not to leave thee, or to return from following after thee: for whither thou goest, I will go; and where thou lodgest, I will lodge: thy people shall be my people, and thy God my God:

She achieved all this by a heart that was determined to follow someone whom she had seen God working through. (Ruth 1:15-16)

A background study on Caleb will reveal that he was not from the original Hebrew nation, however he was a person whose heart was given to following with a true spirit of servanthood and following. A close study on him will reveal his faithfulness in his two mentors, Moses and Joshua. This pleased God which is why He said that Caleb was a person with a different spirit. He falls into a category of a kind of people who will lay down their lives, leaving their own belief systems and traditions for the sake of servanthood, hence Caleb is worth mentioning when it comes to those that are found in the history of those that became heroes of faith through following. Let us do an investigation on some of them.

THE HISTORY OF FOLLOWERS OF FAITH

But my servant Caleb, because he had another spirit with him, and hath followed me fully, him will I bring into the land where into he went; and his seed shall possess it. (Numbers 14:24)

Caleb falls into the category of those who became great heroes, his story has a great ending as he became a hero even though he did not belong to the Hebrew tribe. He was an outsider who became a disciple of Moses and found favour before God. He was given a prophecy by Moses that God was going to give him the land.

And Moses sware on that day, saying, Surely the land whereon thy feet have trodden shall be thine inheritance, and thy children's for ever, because thou hast wholly followed the LORD my God (Joshua 14:9)

Further study of Caleb's life reveals that after the servant of Lord, Moses, died he went to Joshua and reminded him of the prophecy that was given to him when he was in his early forties. It concerned the land that God intended to give him. Joshua was now the leader and he pointed out to him that he had a pending prophecy concerning the land. One of the most profound elements of his prophecy was that God gave him the land because he fully followed Him. His unwavering faith and dedication when others were unfaithful gave him favour before God.

FOLLOWERS POSSESS A DIFFERENT KIND OF SPIRIT

Great followers wholeheartedly pursue their assignments with their hearts completely surrendered to their God. In the case of Caleb, we see from the above passage a reflection of this as God recommends him for having a "different spirit." Following with a "different spirit" requires commitment and forsaking every other thing to pursue the designated goal. In his case, Caleb was a God chaser and his target was the Lord's purpose. Whilst some were falling on the way side, others were murmuring, complaining, persecuting and accusing their leader due to their impatience, Caleb fully followed the Lord. This resulted in God saying, "I will bring him to his land." God's promises require commitment. Those that are half committed will never possess their spiritual inheritance. The ability to follow is supernatural, and defined in this scripture as a "different spirit." The rewards of 'following' are unprecedented; Jesus said in the Holy Scriptures:

And these signs shall follow them that believe; In my name shall they cast out devils; they shall speak with new tongues; They shall take up serpents; and if they drink any deadly thing, it shall not hurt them; they shall lay hands on the sick, and they shall recover. (Mark 16:17-18)

These are some of the benefits received by the followers of the heavenly vision. Jesus specified that those that follow him will not follow in vain as they will be accompanied by supernatural activities.

As shown in the scripture above signs and wonders will be their portion; they will cast out devils as well as speak languages that no man taught them. They will also survive poisoning, from food and snakes. We see this when the Apostle Paul was bitten by a poisonous snake and it did not hurt him.

These benefits are endless since the followers have enrolled into a family of the supernatural. This doesn't happen by choice, it's the election of God's grace that draws people into the supernatural walk through following Jesus. These followers become partakers of those promises which are obtained through following Christ, thereby becoming co-laborers with Jesus the supernatural Worker. Jesus was and always will be supernatural. It is clear in Scripture that no one comes to God unless the Spirit of God draws them.

No man can come to me, except the Father which hath sent me draw him: and I will raise him up at the last day. (John 6:44)

Those that have become followers of Jesus will have the rest of their lives packed with wonders as promised by the scripture. This will enable them to live a supernaturally resurrected lifestyle, forever demonstrating His power, and living their lives through him to eternity. His followers are promised signs and wonders in this world and eternal life in the hereafter. The package of the followers as I mentioned earlier on is endless, in his own words Jesus said, "Follow me and I will make you fishers of man."

"And he saith unto them, follow me, and I will make you fishers of men."
(Matthew 4:19)

The Lord Jesus put a great emphasis to those seeking to follow Him. He pointed out that if they followed Him fully they had to pay a price. However, he also revealed the benefits of their following. He said, "I will make you fishers of men". In short, they were going to win men and become influential, they were going to reveal the kingdom of heaven with the confirmation of signs and wonders.

FOLLOWING ACCORDING TO PAUL THE APOSTLE

Paul was a student of 'following'; his journey began in a supernatural way. He was once part of the persecution of the newly emerged Christian faith. Many people were getting saved through this movement. This new message that was previously unknown was attracting people by the thousands, and the Jewish religious council, in the bid to stop this movement, appointed authorities to persecute its adherents. Paul the Apostle, who was called Saul then, while persecuting this Jesus movement met Jesus.

He appeared to him in a supernatural way, revealing to Paul that he had an assignment for him. This is what led to Paul's conversion. He became one of the greatest followers of Christ in the history of Christianity. In the passage below he begins to reveal strategies as a student of "following" and he had experience of the benefits that come through following Jesus Christ. He took the opportunity to share the benefits and blessings to people who followed him. As recorded in the scripture, He strongly urged people to follow him saying,

I urge you, therefore, to imitate me as I imitate Christ.
(1 Corinthians 4:16)

Paul was not being arrogant but was revealing his secret and the benefits that he received by following. He was encouraging his sons to come on board so that they could become the beneficiaries of the supernatural lifestyle. And his words were, "I urge you to imitate me as I imitate Christ".

This scripture shows Paul's views regarding following. The word urge according to the Webster's dictionary means; to press, to push, to drive, to impel, to force onwards. Paul said this based on his experience that following Jesus was worth striving for. Once one has tasted the supernatural, it is difficult to be satisfied with something else as there is nothing that compares favourably with it. In other words, Paul was saying to them, "when I got exposed to the supernatural lifestyle I did not look back, but I kept going forward." When God has given you an appetizer it draws you on, it impels you to get more. It activates your faith and your desire. The purpose of God in revealing himself by way of demonstrating his supernatural acts is so that mankind can experience His nature and His attributes. Paul the Apostle encouraged other people in the Bible. On this occasion, he used the phrase, "imitate me."

Imitate me, just as I also imitate Christ. (1Corinthians 11:1)

Great leaders are great imitators. Paul the Apostle not only told them to imitate him, but he also told them who he was also imitating, and why. He followed Jesus and saw the results that are attached to following Jesus, now he was telling his followers what he had discovered. If you are following the supernatural Jesus there is an impartation of spiritual grace and gifts that are resident in the supernatural move of God.

One of the ways supernatural transfers occur is through imitating. There is nothing that is new under the sun, we are all copies of one another, and of those that were before us. History shows us if we apply the same principles they applied we are bound to get similar results. Paul was sharing the depth of his understanding that to have success, you must be willing to follow someone, who has a good track record. Hence in the case of Jesus, he was urging his disciples to follow him so that they can be powerful.

The DNA of the supernatural is found in Jesus. Paul in the above scripture used the word 'urge,' to motivate his spiritual sons to do the same thing he did. The word 'urge' from the Webster's dictionary is as follows: "to present in an urgent manner; to press upon attention; to insist upon; as, to urge an argument; to urge the necessity of a case." He emphasised the necessity of them following him, and imitating him because he had seen the value and the benefits derived from it.

Be ye followers of me, even as I also am of Christ. (1 Corinthians 11:1)

Paul the Apostle on another occasion gave a similar instruction when he said: "imitate me". He was putting an emphasis on the fact that what he did could be achieved by them. Greatness produces greatness. The supernatural is transferable grace that is released by those that carry it; they release it from divine impartation. Hence, he was urging them and instructing them to join him, so that they could be partakers of the same grace of the supernatural. Spiritual gifts can be imparted; they are transferable as Paul the apostle explains it in the following passage:

For I long to see you, that I may impart unto you some spiritual gift, to the end ye may be established; (Romans 1:11)

One of the reasons he gave was that it will, in turn, cause them to be established. Spiritual gifts are transferred to edify and strengthen those that are part of the Kingdom.

He said unto them, Have ye received the Holy Ghost since ye believed? And they said unto him, we have not so much as heard whether there be any Holy Ghost. (Acts 19:2)

Here are some of Paul's the Apostle's supernatural achievements:

I have fought a good fight, I have finished my course, and I have kept the faith: (2 Timothy 4:7)

Paul was a spiritual warrior, and in his own words he said to his spiritual son, Timothy, "I fought a good fight". The fight that Paul was referring to was not a physical fight, but a spiritual one. When it comes to spiritual matters, the Bible declares, "we wrestle not against flesh and blood," which simply means it's not a natural fight. If it's a not natural fight it's a supernatural fight. In supernatural matters Paul excelled, hence when he said to his spiritual sons "I urge you to imitate me, or follow me" he was speaking from a position of strength, not weakness. Not from a natural point of view but a supernatural one. He had a proven track record.

Time after time, ministry challenges presented themselves before him and he didn't give in or give up, he fought through as a true soldier committed to the victory, hence he said: "I have kept the faith". This is the life of a man who had the qualities of persistence and continuity; he didn't allow satan's forces, tactics, and pressure to defeat him, in other words, he did not blow his gasket or throw in the towel. When such a leader says imitate me, he is worthy to be imitated, because such an instruction must never be taken lightly, it carries great value and will benefit whoever applies it to their life.

For I am the least of the apostles, that am not meet to be called an apostle, because I persecuted the church of God. But by the grace of God, I am what I am: and his grace which was be- stowed upon me was not in vain, but I laboured more abundantly than they all: yet not I, but the grace of

God which was with me. (1 Corinthians 15:9 -12)

Let us continue to look at some of Paul's achievements or activities of the supernatural in his life.

It is encouraging that Paul, the apostle, does not put emphasis on himself as a person or on his intellectual capability and natural abilities, or anything else that can be attributed to his achievements. When he stated in the scripture above that "I am least of the apostles," such a position is self-describing the calibre of the man who is worth following. His level of humility says it all. He is not only saying he was the least of the apostles he alluded to his past activities which were surrounded by darkness.
These are confirmed by the blood of the saints, revealing the fact that his former activities caused the deaths of people such as Stephen, the martyr. He was a man with a testimony of what the grace of God can do, transformed from being a murderer to a supernatural spiritual worker. According to his own words, "it was by the grace of God that I laboured and excelled" beyond even those that had a clean and better past. His record did not prevent him from being used in the supernatural. The grace of God qualifies people to do the works of God; it's not by their works, their past or present abilities, but it's only by the grace of God. He said he persecuted the church before his conversion, but he goes on to point out the supernatural transformation that made him who he became. He strongly emphasized that he laboured more than them all. In other words, even though Paul came last, the amount of his labour was paramount, and he credits it to the grace that was upon his life. Allow me to say that grace is supernatural; his natural abilities his background, his previous

engagements did not qualify him to achieve even half of the things he achieved. Paul's curriculum vitae was fully loaded with testimonies of the supernatural abilities of God.

The passage below in the book of Acts recorded some of the activities of the supernatural that took place during Paul's ministry. This serves as full proof that Paul's following Jesus had confirmation at every angle and that miracles do follow them that believe in the Lord Jesus Christ.

PAUL RAISES THE DEAD TO LIFE

And there sat in a window a certain young man named Eutychus, being fallen into a deep sleep: and as Paul was long preaching, he sunk dow with sleep, and fell down from the third loft, and was taken up dead. And Paul went down, and fell on him, and embracing him said, Trouble not yourselves; for his life is in him. When he, therefore, was come up again, and had broken bread, and eaten, and talked a long while, even till break of day, so he departed. And they brought the young man alive, and were not a little comforted. (Acts 20: 9-12)

This recorded incident refers to a person who was listening to Paul's preaching and fell from the window, and died. Paul prayed and brought him back to life. That is a supernatural display of the resurrection power of Jesus.

PAUL SUPERNATURALLY DEFENDS HIMSELF BEFORE THE KING

Then Agrippa said unto Paul, Thou art per- mitted to speak for thyself. Then Paul stretched forth the hand, and answered for himself: I think myself happy, king Agrippa, because I shall answer for myself this day before thee touching all the things whereof I am accused of the Jews: Especially because I know thee to be expert in all customs and questions which are among the Jews: wherefore I beseech thee to hear me patiently. (Acts 26:1-3)

Above is another recorded incident in the books of Acts concerning Paul the apostle. He was apprehended and brought before the courts of Justice for preaching the gospel. He appeared before King Agrippa and began to defend himself. His whole defense rests on the fact he was under supernatural inspiration, and even while he was speaking he pointed out that he got to where he was by way of a spiritual encounter that occurred to him on his way to Damascus.

Whereupon, O king Agrippa, I was not disobedient unto the heavenly vision (Acts 26:19)

He refers to it as a 'heavenly vision' and told King Agrippa he couldn't ignore it. Again, when Paul was saying 'imitate me' he had a handful of reasons why, such as raising the dead, healing the sick, casting out of devils and won court cases supernaturally. In view of the scripture below, it confirms beyond a shadow of doubt that the man who urged and instructed his followers to follow him was a man tried and tested in every sense.

Not only was he a fighter, he was pushed, and stretched beyond human capacity and his survival was proof of the supernatural working in his life.

A BRIEF SYNOPSIS OF HIS JOURNEY ACCOMPANIED BY THE SUPERNATURAL ACTIVITIES

Thrice was I beaten with rods, once was I stoned, thrice I suffered shipwreck, a night and a day I have been in the deep;
(2 Corinthians 11:25)

And when Paul had gathered a bundle of sticks and laid them on the fire, there came a viper out of the heat and fastened on his hand. And when the barbarians saw the venomous beast hang on his hand, they said among themselves, No doubt this man is a murderer, whom, though he hath escaped the sea, yet vengeance suffereth not to live. And he shook off the beast into the fire, and felt no harm. (Acts 28: 3-5)

His supernatural survival from viper's poison was not due to a natural ability and this shows this man could impart much to those who follow.

REFLECTION AND PRAYER ACTIVATION

1. Caleb had a __________ spirit that led him to follow , This resulted in God promising to __________________.

2. What are the signs that ____________those that believe.

3. Paul recommends that you _________him as he _________ Christ.

4. The result of this following is found in 2 Timothy 4:7. List the three benefits in this verse.

1. ______________ 2. ____________________ 3. ______________

5. Jesus told Peter if he follows Him he will become a ________________________________.

1. Numbers 14:24 [KVJ]
2. Mark 16:17-18 [KVJ]
3. 1 Corinthians 11:1 [KVJ]
4. 2 Timothy 4:7 [KVJ]
5. Matthew 4:19 [KVJ]

PRAYER

Lord give me a heart to follow like Caleb wholeheartedly and unwavering, may I live to please you and pursue your purposes all the days of my life. And may I have all the signs of a true follower of Christ, and may I be a true apostolic disciple who follows only those that follow Christ. Make me a good fighter, a good finisher that I may be able to keep my faith in you Lord. May I be productive in the kingdom of God and be the one who fishes man for the kingdom of God just as Jesus said.

CHAPTER 3

SUPERNATURAL KINGDOM DEMONSTRATORS

The first [a]account I made, Theophilus, was continuous report] about all the things that Jesus began to do and to [b]teach 2 until the day when He ascended to heaven, after He had by the Holy Spirit given instruction to the apostles (special messengers) whom He had chosen. 3 To these [men] He also showed Himself alive after His suffering [in Gethsemane and on the cross], by [a series of] many infallible proofs and unquestionable demonstrations, appearing to them over a period of forty days and talking to them about the things concerning the kingdom of God. (Acts 1:1-3 AMP)

From day one of Jesus' ministry on earth, he demonstrated the power of the kingdom of God with undisputable proofs followed with miracles, signs, and wonders. One of the characteristics that marked his preaching was the supernatural manifestation of the power of God that accompanied his ministry, his lifestyle and his Character also embodied the true evidence that he was indeed the son of the living God.

Ye men of Israel, hear these words; Jesus of Nazareth, a man approved of God among you by miracles and wonders and signs, which God did by him in the midst of you, as ye yourselves also know:
Him, being delivered by the determinate counsel and foreknowledge of God, ye have taken, and by wicked hands have crucified and slain:
(Acts 2:22)

There was a clear distinction that He was a true representative of a Kingdom that was far superior to religion or any other cult or belief system that has ever been known to man. He performed supernatural deeds beyond a shadow of a doubt that confirmed that the gospel He preached was indeed the gospel of the Kingdom of God. His preaching and His doctrine were so pure that wherever He went it carried proof. He preached repentance from sin and introduced the kingdom of heaven that it was now available to those that believed in the good news that he was promulgating.

From that time Jesus began to preach, and to say, Repent: for the kingdom of heaven is at hand. (Matthew 4:17)

The kingdom of God is not merely about preaching or theological presentations, nor is it about intellectual speeches that do not carry any proof or demonstration of the kingdom of God.

And Jesus went about all Galilee, teaching in their synagogues, and preaching the gospel of the kingdom, and healing all manner of sickness and all manner of disease among the people. (Matthew 4:23)

Here is the question that one should be asking, "What is the kingdom of God?" What should one's expectation be at the mention of the word kingdom of God. At the mention of the kingdom of God, there must be notable proof of signs and miracles as evidence that proves and supports with a clear distinction that indeed this is nothing but the kingdom of God.

For the kingdom of God is not meat and drink; but righteousness, and peace, and joy in the Holy Ghost (Romans 14:17)

If we answer the question of what is the kingdom of God based on the scripture, we get a brief explanation of what is found in the kingdom of God. The Kingdom of God entails righteousness, and peace and joy that is brought about by the Holy Ghost. In short; where the kingdom of God, is people are in right standing with God; they are at peace; not in chaos or anarchy; they are flourishing in the joy which is provided by the Holy Ghost. One of the explanations of the kingdom of God from the Old Testament point of view is that children of Israel when God moved among them demonstrating His supernatural power.
According to Paul the Apostle in the scripture below, he made it clear that his preaching was not based on fancy words or philosophies of man, but it was based on the demonstration of the spirit of God.

And my speech and my preaching was not with enticing words of man's wisdom, but in demontration of the Spirit and of power: (1 Corinthians 2:4)

Paul's words support that the preaching of the gospel should always be accompanied with demonstrations; Signs, wonders, and miracles are an endorsement that the kingdom of God has been presented, and that God agrees with the preacher. The opposite is equally true; let us look at what is not the kingdom of God.

For the kingdom of God is not in word, but in power. (1Corinthians 4:20)

There are so many people who claim to be in the kingdom of God but have nothing to show for it. Others will have something to show, even though it is not the real thing. God always backs His preaching with indisputable proofs, and miracles that are genuine; they are righteous and pure. They will not have any question marks because the tragedy of the time we live in is that there are counterfeits. There are generic preachers who claim to have the kingdom, and they are deceiving many. It is easy to distinguish them because their motives are not right; most of what they do is for self-enrichment. As I said there are generic spirits out there and one needs to distinguish between truth and a lie. Jesus forewarned that there will be many that will come claiming to be the Christ; they will be saying the kingdom of God is here; He said don't believe them. The reason why they should not be believed is because they don't have the full proof of the kingdom of God.

Then if any man shall say unto you, Lo, here is Christ, or there; believe it not. For there shall arise false Christs, and false prophets, and shall shew great signs and wonders; insomuch that, if it were possible, they shall deceive the very elect. (Matthew 24: 23-24)

A recap on what Paul the Apostle was saying that his preaching was based on the demonstration of the power of God. His statement was directed to the people at Corinth who were the philosophers of their time. They spent most of their time entertained by engaging people who had a different point of view or philosophy. These were the people that Paul was addressing and his emphasis was to them. He declared that when he came to them, he did not engage them based on the wisdom of man; but rather on the demonstration of the supernatural power of God. He then goes to explain why he did that in the following verse.

That your faith should not stand in the wisdom of men, but in the power of God. (1 Corinthians 2:5)

He wanted their faith to be based on the power of God versus the philosophies of man. One of the main reasons why God's supernatural power is demonstrated is for people's faith to be established in Him, and not in the words of man. The counterfeits and philosophers want to gain mileage for their own benefit. It has nothing to do with the kingdom of God. Hence Paul educated as he was could have been philosophical but chose not to. He could have used the wisdom of man but did not. He emptied himself and trusted God's supernatural power to be the source that their faith should be established on.

The above scripture seeks to address that it is not theological jargon or empty words of man's wisdom that God uses. He then refers to the fact his entrance among them was accompanied by the demonstration of the power of God.
The people that were referred to in this case were very philosophical and they had itching ears and wanted new philosophies. Every time someone came in and began to speak something new they would feel entertained and want to engage that person, so that they can hear more, then the writer began to say that his approach when he came to them was different, he could have engaged them pound for pound but he refused to do so as seen in the passage above that he said, I didn't want your faith to be grounded in man's ideology but rather in God, how he was going to achieve that was based on the statement that he said "I came demonstrating a kingdom".

And my speech and my preaching was not with enticing words of man's wisdom, but in demonstration of the Spirit and of power
(1 Corinthians 2:4)

The demonstration of the kingdom of our Lord Jesus Christ is supported by the supernatural demonstration of the power of the living God. The writer of the books of the Acts of the Apostles opens his letter with the words, "that Jesus began to do and teach." King Jesus Himself didn't only come with words, even though He was an excellent teacher as seen through the New Testament, spending time in synagogues. He taught with parables and gave quality teachings to His audience and theologians of His time applauded Him for His teaching. They said His teaching was with authority, He was an authority in His time, who taught as one sent from heaven. As one of the speakers said: "You are a teacher that came from heaven". However, despite his teaching abilities, he first demonstrated the supernatural and then taught.

The former treatise have I made, O Theophilus, of all that Jesus began both to do and teach, (Acts 1:1)

THE SUPERNATURAL IS A DIRECT CONFRONTATION WITH SATANS KINGDOM

Demons as well as sickness and diseases, are subject to the supernatural, whenever the supernatural is demonstrated Satan's kingdom falls like lightning. He raised a supernatural team and he imparted his supernatural grace to them sending them in pairs to their first practical supernatural exercise. They came back with a one hundred percent success rate, they had performed everything he had charged them to do. This was what He Himself did involving healing the sick, cleansing the lepers and raising the dead. Jesus Himself confirmed that by what he had seen in the spiritual realm; saying He "saw Satan fall like lightning from heaven".
Upon their return, they brought tremendous testimonies when he asked them to give an account of what they experienced,

And the seventy returned with joy, saying, Lord, even the devils are subject unto us through thy name. And he said unto them, I beheld Satan as lightning fall from heaven. (Luke 10:17)

Their response was that "even the devils are subject to us," This is confirmation that they went with a mandate which had supernatural capabilities.

This in turn caused demonic forces to be subject to them. His team was endowed with supernatural grace to deal with the demonic world, diseases and sicknesses could not outmatch them as they went with His supernatural backup. He confirmed to them what they had experienced; "I saw Satan fall like lightning". Representatives of the kingdom of God are the only ones that can deal with Satan's kingdom to the degree that we saw Jesus and his students display in the above scripture. The kingdom of God is the kingdom of power and is the kingdom of glory. Jesus once said in the scripture below:

But if I with the finger of God cast out devils, no doubt the kingdom of God has come upon you. (Luke 11:20)

Jesus explained that by demonstrating the supernatural He was, in fact, revealing the kingdom of God. His explanation of the kingdom of God was marked by supernatural demonstration. Here is a brief explanation of the kingdom of God. The Kingdom of God speaks of where the king rules and reigns; for example, the universe; the spiritual realm of which God is the acknowledged sovereign. The word 'kingdom' is also made up of two words "king" and "domain"; which means where the king rules and reigns, which also means 'the domain of the king'. The kingdom of God is eternal; His dominion is transgenerational.

The mandate of the kingdom workers was given by Jesus to his disciples as we see in the history of the early church. It is evident that its birthing was confirmed by supernatural activities. It all started with the outpouring of the Holy Spirit accompanied by the evidence of speaking in tongues.

It was a sovereign move of God that was instrumental in the birthing of the church and it brought about amazement in those that witnessed the event. This supernatural occurrence attracted different people. As they listened to them speak in languages they could identify, being spoken by people who had never learnt them they realized it was a supernatural empowerment. Hence, they were amazed, and it also brought the conviction and ultimately a conversion to this new movement. From nothing; the church grew to thousands. It was authentic due to the supernatural endorsement that it demonstrated. At its debut, there was an amazing number of people converted by an inexperienced preacher who came out of the fishing industry. He was an ordinary fisherman whom God supernaturally endowed to preach, and as he spoke, his words were so supernaturally empowered that his audience began to ask him, "What must we do?" He answered and gave them the way forward. He stated that they must 'repent and be saved and be baptized'. He further specifically mentioned if they did so they would receive the supernatural power of the Holy Spirit.

He was confirming that those who came to this newly established faith were going to be filled with the Holy Spirit just as Jesus had promised. And he was extending to them that they won't regret it and it was available to them; even to future generations. The people responded as I said in their numbers. One of the characteristics of the early church was that it became a strong community that grew on a daily basis; a community of people loving; caring and sharing with one another. They experienced what I call a supernatural financial 'injection' which was brought in by those that were well resourced and had become part of the community. They also had become part of the supernatural community that operated in the dimension of supernatural generosity that only God can give. The widows were taken care of, there was no one who lacked anything as the scripture declares:

And all that believed were together, and had all things common; (Act 2:44)

Jesus commanded them to heal the sick, cleanse the lepers raise the dead and preach the gospel. Whatever was demonstrated by the early church reveals the attributes of the kingdom of God. When He gave them this mandate He emphasized that they must demonstrate the kingdom and offer it for free, it's not for sale, he said:

Heal the sick, cleanse the lepers, raise the dead, cast out devils: freely ye have received, freely give. (Matthew 10:8)

REFLECTION AND PRAYER ACTIVATION

1. What did Jesus ___________and preach.

2. Jesus of Nazareth was a man approved of ________________ among you by miracles _____________ and signs.

3. Jesus began to preach and said repent ______________ at hand.

4. Jesus went about all Galilee teaching in their synagogues and the gospel of the kingdom.

5. The kingdom of God is not meat and drink but ____________ and peace and joy in the Holy Ghost.

6. What did he say his preaching was not ______________ wisdom but in demonstration of the Spirit and of power.

7. What did the seventy disciples say upon their return? Even are subject unto us through thy name.

8. What did the believers had in common? And all that believed _______________ all things in common.

9. What did Jesus tell them to do with what they had received?

1. Acts 1:1-3 [AMP]
2. Acts 2:22 [KJV]

3. Matthew 4:17 [KJV]
4. Matthew 4:23 [KJV]
5. Romans 14:17 [KJV]
6. 1Corinthians 2:4 [KJV]
7. Luke 10:17 [KJV]
8. Acts 2:44 [KJV]
9. Matthew 10:8 [KJV]

PRAYER

Lord give me a heart to follow You fully so that I might please You and be filled with the Spirit and become a demonstrator of the kingdom of God. I want Your power to teach and demonstrate. May I be approved of God through miracles, wonders and signs, so that I may preach the gospel of repentance and of the kingdom of God which is full of the power of the Holy Ghost and which is fully demonstrated by the supernatural working of the Holy Ghost and be like the seventy-two that saw the power of Satan fall like lightning. Make me to be part of the community of the believers that share a common faith and that I may freely give of which that was given to me, Amen.

CHAPTER 4

SUPERNATURAL WARFARE

We live in a world that has a great history of wars, these wars have been fought over time and these great wars have seen other nations prevailing over others. History has it, there was world war one, world war two and we might be on the verge of world war three, there is current information with conclusive evidence that suggests that other nations have now developed nuclear weapons that can travel the distance and are armed with warheads that are capable of destroying entire cities and nations. In the past we have heard of wars that almost brought other nations close to extinction such as the war between the United States and Vietnam. From time to time some powerful nations have always built nuclear weapons that can outsmart other nations and some of these weapons can destroy the whole world by just a click of a button. This is just but an indication that just as there are natural wars there are also spiritual wars. The war of good versus evil, Satan and his evil forces against God's holy army. As the Bible indicates the devil came to steal, to kill and to destroy. Satan's wars are at work day and night to separate man from God to destroy his very existence if need be. Jesus said he came that we may have life and that we may have abundant life.

The thief cometh not, but for to steal, and to kill, and to destroy: I am come that they might have life, and that they might have it more abundantly. (John 10:10 KJV)

There is a spiritual warfare that is going on out there even though we may not see it with our natural eyes but its effects are real. The book of John has this to say:

The wind blows where it wishes and you hear its sound, but you do not know where it is coming from and where it is going; so it is with everyone who is born of the Spirit. (John 3:8 AMP)

Spiritual warfare cannot be perceived with a natural eye however we can feel its effects and see its manifestations. You have to be in the spirit in order to discern what's going on in the spirit.
Spiritual warfare is not fiction; just as there is a natural world, there is also a spiritual one. Most of the things that we see in the natural world begin in the spirit. God is Spirit and the Bible says He must be worshipped in spirit and in truth. We are His children and the whole world is full of his people. We are created in the image of God and in His likeness. Part of our makeup is from the earth, as we see in the scriptures that God made man from dust, and another part of us is the spirit, which is the image of God, another word for 'image' is a shadow.

And the Lord God formed man of the dust of the ground, and breathed

into his nostrils the breath of life; and man became a living soul.
(Genesis 2:7)

A man is a tripartite being who is a spirit, and has a soul and body. Our spirit man lives forever, our bodies have a limited lifespan, they were created for this earth, and after a while, return to the earth from which we came from, but our spirit came from God and it will live forever because God is eternal, therefore, the spirit of a man is eternal. On the other hand, angels are spirits, they are ministering spirits whom God created to assist those who are heirs of salvation. They are not seen by the natural eye but they are real. They can see us and help us but we can't usually see them; they are spirit beings and they fall into two categories; the elect angels and the fallen angels. Who are the fallen angels? Lucifer is their chief, who is also known as Satan, a fallen angel, who was one of the archangels in heaven responsible for the worship ministry until iniquity was found in him. This simply means he had a wrong agenda and was not serving the purposes of God with a clean heart. God had to fire him. Upon being fired, he led a third of angels astray who were cast out, or, fired for collaborating with him. Lucifer and his fallen angels are the ones that constitute the category of 'fallen angels'.

The whole spiritual warfare is fought against Satan in collaboration with his fallen angels by those that are in the kingdom of God.

For we wrestle not against flesh and blood, but against principalities, against powers, against the rulers of the darkness of this world, against spiritual wickedness in high places. (Ephesians6:12)

The above scripture describes the fallen angels as principalities and powers in heavenly places; so spiritual warfare is in a realm where the devil has organized himself and he has a principality with different departments designed to frustrate and to bring the kingdom of God into disrepute.
He works hand in hand with the fallen angels to afflict mankind through various principalities.
Paul the Apostle had a vast knowledge of spiritual warfare, hence when he wrote to the Ephesians he elaborated on matters pertaining to spiritual warfare, such as where it is fought and the principalities involved.

If after the manner of men I have fought with beasts at Ephesus, what advantageth it me, if the dead rise not? let us eat and drink; for to morrow we die. (1 Corinthians 15: 32)

The apostle Paul had something to say concerning a scenario he encountered in Ephesus. He again speaks about his involvement in a fight and this time he uses the word 'beasts', he said I have fought with 'beasts'. Satan uses demonic influences to resist the workers of the kingdom of God; as I have alluded before that Satan and his fallen angels are spirits. The other word for them is 'demons', which are spirits without bodies. Spirits don't have bodies to express themselves, therefore, they possess people and carry out their evil agenda through human vessels, or, whatever has a body as they cannot function on the earth because the earth was designed for those that have bodies.
Jesus the Christ during the days of His ministry came to a city called Gadah; where a man was possessed with a legion of demons. Before He

delivered that man, the demons asked Him if they could go into the pigs. That story serves as a confirmation that demons can possess human beings as well as animals. This earth was not designed for spirits, human beings are the legal occupants that were designed to function on this earth, and however, satan influences them to gain permission into their bodies. He then makes their bodies express his evil intentions and carries them out through the bodies of those that give him permission. So, Paul experienced evil people who were possessed by demons and he describes them in the scripture quoted above that at Ephesus he fought with beasts. When a normal human being is possessed by an evil spirit it can be a hundred times more powerful than it ought to be. Throughout history, some world leaders were possessed by Satan carried out evil atrocities that affected mankind. Human beings possessed by the devil are worse than wild beasts. Paul's description seeks to address that the warfare we engage in is equal to fighting with wild beasts. His experience at Ephesus gave him that conclusion.

Certain behavioral tendencies that are animal like in nature are a clear indication that there is a spiritual influence behind it, it is under that scenario that Paul was describing his spiritual experience with those that resisted him at Ephesus as beasts. In many passages of the Bible similar reference are found even John the Baptist in his preaching referred a group of people as a generation of vipers. In the book of Jude certain characteristics are referred to as brute beast. In my personal experience I have seen people who were under the influences of demonic possessions with facial expressions similar to animals and some released animal sounds. In the spiritual realm the devil can demonstrate himself as animals of different species.

IN THIS WARFARE THERE ARE VARIOUS WEAPONS

For the weapons of our warfare are not carnal, but mighty through God to the pulling down of strong holds, Casting down imaginations, and every high thing that exalteth itself against the knowledge of God, and bringing into captivity every thought to the obedience of Christ;
(2 Corinthians 10:4-5)

This scripture above seeks to address the fact that we are involved in a warfare, and it clearly reveals that this warfare is not a natural warfare but a spiritual one. Let us look at the situation involving Elisha and the young man in the Bible.

And Elisha prayed, and said, Lord, I pray thee, open his eyes, that he may see. And the Lord opened the eyes of the young man; and he saw: and, behold, the mountain was full of horses and chariots of fire round about Elisha. (2 Kings 6:17)

Above is the prayer of Elisha. He and the young man were surrounded by an army that outnumbered them. Prophets and servants of God often found themselves being resisted because demons have an agenda to fight them and stop them by any means available. If they can find a way, they will eliminate them by murdering them. Elisha was in a place where he and his servants were being resisted, hence this young man raised a genuine concern. He wanted to know how they were going to get out of it alive.

Elisha was the prophet of God had spiritual insight which was from his prophetic grace, or, anointing that allowed him to view things in the spiritual realm. He did not waste time to try and elaborate on this to the young man, but rather prayed for the young man's spiritual eyes to be open. This prayer was answered and the young man could see the angelic forces surrounding them, together with an escort of chariots of fire. Allow me to say that in today's terms this would be like a heavenly army with tanks that came to their aid to fight the spiritual battle for them. There are many references in the Bible that speak of chariots and horses and I believe this scripture confirms the fact that in the warfare we are involved in there are weapons, horses and chariots that are supernatural; These are available to God's servants and people today. They are dispatched supernaturally by God to help his people when in trouble. Hence, Elisha was not panicking like the young man, because he knew that greater was He who was with them than the enemy that was coming against them.

ANGELIC INVOLVEMENT IN SPIRITUAL WARFARE

And they smote the men that were at the door of the house with blindness, both small and great: so that they wearied themselves to find the door.
(Genesis 19:11)

Abraham prayed for Lot and God sent angels to deliver Lot; and when the angels arrived at Lot's house, the people of Sodom tried to resist Lot and the angels stroke them with blindness. Here is another classic demonstration of how the angels stroke those that wanted to afflict Lot with blindness that they could not see. Angels have supernatural abilities that can stop the track of human beings without them seeing it. Angels can stop accidents and can fight in ways that are indescribable, they have incredible supernatural abilities.

There are angels in the army of God and there are weapons in the army of God that are spiritual and not carnal. A further consideration of the story will reveal what the angels did to those that were coming against the servants of God. There are forces that come against us that we don't see, there are forces that fight them on our behalf that we don't see, they fight for us, and the fact that they are not revealed to our natural eye does not mean they are not at work. We should take comfort in the fact that God is the God of the armies of heaven. Angels always fight, there's a great amount of supporting scriptures throughout the Bible that reveals their involvement when the saints got into situations that required God's intervention.

HERE IS ANOTHER SUPERNATURAL INVOLVEMENT IN THE CASE OF PETER

And, behold, the angel of the Lord came upon him, and a light shined in the prison: and he smote Peter on the side, and raised him up, saying, Arise up quickly. And his chains fell off from his hands. (Acts 12:7)

Another classic intervention that an angel appeared in prison to rescue Peter. The assignment of angels is to fight for the saints, they are equipped with tremendous power and abilities they can step in and do the unspeakable, provide reinforcement and work deliverance for God's people in times of need, and they were created for such.

But to which of the angels said he at any time, Sit on my right hand, until I make thine enemies thy footstool? Are they not all ministering spirits, sent forth to minister for them who shall be heirs of salvation?
(Hebrews 1: 13-14)

The above emphasizes that angels are ministering spirits that are assigned to minister to those who are heirs of salvation. There is another account that involves one angel that was assigned to fight the Assyrian army overnight; the angel single-handedly killed 72 thousand soldiers, which reveals how powerful angels can be. The good part of that story is that this fight was a supernatural one, showing God's care for His children who are part of His kingdom. Angels are not a fairytale that exists in the comic books, they are so real they exist today; they are not only found in ancient stories of God's dealings with mankind; they are part of our daily lives.

And it came to pass that night, that the angel of the LORD went out, and smote in the camp of the Assyrians a hundred fourscore and five thousand: and when they arose early in the morning, behold, they were all dead corpses. (2 Kings 19:35)

Wherever angels fight they are known for great results. Angels are not foolish, they are wise and they know far more of what is hidden to the human mind, their intellect is beyond comprehension.

To fetch about this form of speech hath thy servant Joab done this thing:

and my lord is wise, according to the wisdom of an angel of God, to know all things that are in the earth. (2 Samuel 14:20)

Thou madest him a little lower than the angels; thou crownedst him with glory and honour, and didst set him over the works of thy hands: (Hebrews 2:7)

THE GIDEON FACTOR

Gideon was sent by God to fight the Midianites, as the Chief Commander of the army he began to prepare a huge force to go and fight.

And the LORD said unto Gideon, The people that are with thee are too many for me to give the Midianites into their hands, lest Israel vaunt themselves against me, saying, Mine own hand hath saved me. (Judges 7:2)

God spoke to him, to his surprise, he was instructed to downsize the number. Upon downsizing he was told that the number was still not acceptable, so the number went from 30000 to 10000 then ultimately to 300. God fights supernaturally, the Bible calls Him the Lord God of Hosts, which means the God of the armies of heaven, which means from heaven He commands His troops.

As for our redeemer, the Lord of hosts is his name, the Holy One of Israel. (Isaiah 47:4)

Every time God does something He wants to get the Glory. No one should claim victory at God's expense. God does not answer by crowd he is the self-existing God. When everyone seems to have gone away, when at times you feel that you are all alone, and human systems have failed you or have let you down, then watch God. When Jesus was facing one of the darkest moments of His life He forewarned His followers that they were going to abandon Him and leave Him alone. This was in spite of Peter insisting he would not. This came to pass and Jesus was left alone; He was left alone at the mercy of those who wanted Him crucified. This in spite of Jesus asking His followers to stand with Him in prayer because of the tragedy of the hour, the betrayal, the trial and His crucifixion. They indicated their willingness to participate in praying and He warned them that their weakness was their flesh, or, naturally they could not do it.

Regardless of Him urging them to pray because of His foreknowledge of what was lying ahead of Him, they still found that the Spirit was willing but the flesh was weak.

Watch and pray, that ye enter not into temptation: the spirit indeed is willing, but the flesh is weak. (Matthew 26:41)

There are times when we don't get the physical support, the natural support from those that you think might be your closest friends. It is in these lonely moments, in these alone moments that the supernatural hand of God is manifested. Before they captured Jesus in the garden of Gethsemane the supernatural presence of God was so real that when they tried to draw close to arrest Him, they all fell to the ground. Peter tried to engage them 'naturally', but Jesus understood spiritual warfare, and he didn't respond with physical fighting. On the cross Jesus hung alone even saying to His Father, "Why have you forsaken me?" It seemed that God had forsaken His only Son, on the contrary, there was a tremendous victory that had been won in the spiritual realm; God was busy conquering Satan when Jesus was feeling like He was alone. There is a familiar saying that says with God a minority is a majority.

And about the ninth hour, Jesus cried with a loud voice, saying, Eli, Eli, lama sabachthani? that is to say, My God, my God, why hast thou forsaken me? (Matthew 27:46)

It was during that moment that Jesus was saying, "I am alone", that God was winning the whole world.

O wit, that God was in Christ, reconciling the world unto himself, not imputing their trespasses unto them; and hath committed unto us the word of reconciliation. (2 Corinthians 5:19)

Jesus was forsaken so that the world would be accepted. This the highest order of warfare, it is through the cross that Jesus conquered the world, the flesh and the Devil. It was at the cross where He made the final declaration and decreed that it is finished. The death, the burial and the resurrection of Jesus the Christ were the final supernatural warfare for the salvation of human beings at its best. Through His death redemption came, through His resurrection eternal life came. Jesus set the pace of spiritual warfare, He came to fight the Devil once and for all and conquered him.

When Jesus, therefore, had received the vinegar, he said, it is finished: and he bowed his head, and gave up the ghost. (John 19:30)

Separated from the crowd to stand alone, He conquered death, sin, the flesh and the devil. One of the principles of how a God-led spiritual warfare is conducted is always 'through God and the minority'. This is seen in the case of Gideon when God told him that the people that were with him were too many for Him to give the Midianites in his hand, "lest Israel vaunt and say they have done it in their own strength."
Supernatural warfare strategies that God reveals are seen throughout the Bible, and He often sends signals to the enemy's camp in order to cause the enemy to be afraid. In the account of Gideon, God hinted that Gideon go secretly to listen to the conversation of his enemy, in order to confirm to him that spiritual warfare was already in motion in his favor.

And it was so when Gideon heard the telling of the dream, and the interpretation thereof, that he worshipped, and returned into the host of Israel, and said, Arise; for the LORD hath delivered into your hand the host of Midian. (Judges 7:15)

Upon going he overheard one of them narrating his dream and the interpretation thereof that the sword of Gideon was going to win the battle. A further follow up on the story Gideon employed the same interpretation as he shouted going against the Midianites using the words that spoke about this sword of Gideon. It was through the word, the sword of the spirit; when Gideon heard it he received confidence that the battle had been won spiritually, and it propelled him to go and encourage his camp in spite of their number. He told them to know that God had already settled the victory in the spiritual realm. The word of God is quick, sharp, and powerful. When we fight with the promise of God nothing can stand in our way.

For the word of God is quick, and powerful, and sharper than any two-edged sword, piercing even to the dividing asunder of soul and spirit, and of the joints and marrow, and is a discerner of the thoughts and intents of the heart. (Hebrews 4:12)

In this we note that God comes through supernaturally so that He gets the glory, He is known for providing specific details even on the ambushes on how the warfare must be carried out.

JOSHUA AND THE CAPTAIN OF THE HEAVENLY ARMY

Joshua, Loose thy shoe from off thy foot; for the place whereon thou standest is holy. And Joshua did so. (Joshua 5:15)

In the passage above, Joshua experienced a supernatural encounter with the Captain of the Armies of Heaven. The supernatural warfare that we are engaged in is so organized that it's led by captains and different ranks, just like in the natural army. In this encounter, Joshua is instructed to take off his shoes. It is a common practice that junior ranked officers take orders from their seniors. In this encounter, Joshua was the leader who met his Chief in Command of the supernatural armies of heaven. His command to Joshua was specifically to take off his shoes. Taking off the shoes speaks of a lifestyle of holiness that makes spiritual warfare successful.

Many have been compromised because they tried to fight in the army of God when their lifestyles were questionable and therefore the enemy took them out. You can never lead in the army of God when you are not at a place of holiness. It is impossible for one to take someone where they are not, it will be hypocritical, it would reflect the attitude of 'do as I say and not as I do'. Holiness and spiritual warfare work hand in hand. This encounter of the Lord was to provide Joshua with warfare strategies on how to conquer and possess Jericho.

And it came to pass, when all the kings of the Amorites, which were on the side of Jordan westward, and all the kings of the Canaanites, which were by the sea, heard that the LORD had dried up the waters of Jordan from before the children of Israel, until we were passed over, that their heart melted, neither was their spirit in them anymore, because of the children of Israel. (Joshua 5:1)

DAVID'S SUPERNATURAL APPROACH TO WARFARE

A study on some classic battles that were fought by the men of the Bible, it is interesting to note that David is one of the great characters that stand out. He was in a class of his own. His unique methods and style of warfare were supernatural and no one can dispute that his battles were fought through divine assistance. For example, when the entire nation had come to a deadlock, when they did not know how to forge ahead, they had no clue in how to deal with a giant by the name of Goliath, David was the only one who seemed to know how to navigate ahead and came up with what I want to call in this book the Five Stone strategy.
It was during the reign of King Saul that the Philistines came to provoke his army by asking them to come fight with one of their giants as seen in the scripture below

And the Philistines stood on a mountain on the one side, and Israel stood on a mountain on the other side: and there was a valley between them. And there went out a champion out of the camp of the Philistines, named Goliath, of Gath, whose height was six cubits and a span. And he had a helmet of brass upon his head, and he was armed with a coat of mail, and the weight of the coat was five thousand shekels of brass. And he had greaves of brass upon his legs, and a target of brass between his shoulders. And the staff of his spear was like a weaver's beam, and his spear's head weighed six hundred shekels of iron: and one bearing a shield went before him. And he stood and cried unto the armies of Israel, and said unto them, Why are ye come out to set your battle in array? am not I a Philistine, and ye servants to Saul? choose you a man for you, and let him come down to me. If he be able to fight with me and to kill me, then will we be your servants: but if I prevail against him, and kill him, then shall ye be our servants, and serve us. (1Samuel 17:3-9)

The Philistines presented a Champion, a giant who was extraordinarily huge so that in the natural no one would dare come face to face with him. Anyone in his right mind would say that it would amount to suicide to face Goliath. The entire camp of the Israelite army was devastated and they could not respond to the challenge in front of them. This is when David showed up. This provocation came to his ears and he responded in the following manner. First of all, David wanted to know is there a reward for someone who could take care of this reproach.

And David spake to the men that stood by him, saying, What shall be done to the man that killeth this Philistine, and taketh away the reproach from Israel? for who is this uncircumcised Philistine, that he should defy the armies of the living God? (1 Samuel 17:26)

I don't think he was trying to get a position or a reward; rather he was making sure that the right principle was shown. Someone who would take the lead under these circumstances should atleast be acknowledged as a national hero. The Bible speaks of a worker who is worthy of His hire and after getting the right answer his motivation was in place. He then was ready to go and face the champion. The question of his military background came up. He had his own résumé that he presented before the king, the Chief in Command of the armies of Israel. King Saul was by this time desperate and found himself listening to a non-military person with zero military background telling him he was the man for the job. This is what David had to say to the king:

And David said unto Saul, Thy servant kept his father's sheep, and there came a lion, and a bear, and took a lamb out of the flock: And I went out after him, and smote him, and delivered it out of his mouth: and when he arose against me, I caught him by his beard, and smote him, and slew him. Thy servant slew both the lion and the bear: and this uncircumcised Philistine shall be as one of them, seeing he hath defied the armies of the living God. (1 Samuel 17:34-36)

When asked by the king how he was going to take care of the situation at hand. David alluded to the fact that even though he was not a trained soldier he had dealt with some giants in the past. He referred to a lion, a real lion, and a bear, a real bear. David knew a supernatural God that he had experienced during his time of shepherding. Supernatural warfare was not new to him and he knew the God who was capable of giving him victory, and why He was capable and how He loved to fight for His people. It was this response that caused King Saul to give the green light to showcase his supernatural approach to this reproach of that day. However, King Saul wanted to offer him assistance as an experienced commander who was familiar with this kind of setting, because naturally, you don't go to fight without a shield, a spear, or, a sword. This was his offer.

And Saul said unto David, Go, and the LORD be with thee. And Saul armed David with his armour, and he put a helmet of brass upon his head; also he armed him with a coat of mail. And David girded his sword upon his armour, and he assayed to go; for he had not proved it. And David said unto Saul, I cannot go with these; for I have not proved them. And David put them off him. (1 Samuel 17:38)

From the scripture we hear that David refused to put on the armor of the king even though in the natural it made sense. He said to the king, "I have not proved this", it seems to suggest that David had his own approved supernatural warfare strategy, his warfare strategy was a supernatural one. As alluded to in the above scriptures this was a man who had prevailed fighting without a sword, without a shield and without armor. How did he do it? He could only have done it through divine assistance and he was saying that it was a proven strategy. He was going to go with God and stick to His plan. He refused the natural conventional method of warfare and went with the spiritual supernatural unconventional method. He counted this as a spiritual warfare and he wanted to approach it spiritually. Supernatural warfare has no formula, it is spontaneous, it is God led, and you listen to what God is saying at that given time and execute your strategy as the Spirit of God leads. On the other hand Goliath, the champion, did the same old thing; someone carried his shield and he carried a spear and to his surprise, a young man, not even a giant was coming to him with a sling and stones. Supernatural warfare is not based on looks, it is based on the strength of the God you represent. The giant spoke curses ignorant of the God of the supernatural who was represented by David. David did not keep quiet either. He also spoke out and introduced the God of the armies of Israel; this is what he had to say.

Then said David to the Philistine, Thou comest to me with a sword, and with a spear, and with a shield: but I come to thee in the name of the

LORD of hosts, the God of the armies of Israel, whom thou hast defied. *[1 Samuel 17:45)*

In supernatural warfare, it is important to respond to the enemy and never keep quiet. You cannot employ a quiet diplomacy strategy. When you speak the word of God it has power to stop the enemy and to create supernatural results. Shout out, speak out, and let the redeemed of the Lord say so. David overcame the giant with five stones and a sling. What a supernatural way to win; by just swinging the sling he became victorious. From that day on his name was written in annals of the history of Israel, as a spiritual warfare hero who brought pride and praise to the glory of God.

THE FOUR LEPERS' FACTOR

God has his own chosen warriors whom he appoints to fight his battles, they don't choose God they are chosen by Him. He hand-picks them, prepares them, and sends them to fight in a supernatural way that will give him the glory and the honor. God is always unpredictable and the results are always supernatural. He sometimes answers through fire, through rain, through thunder, but sometimes He answers through a still small voice. As I said before His methods are unpredictable, He sometimes answers now or he may choose to answer after a while and sometimes after a long time. Nevertheless, when He answers it's always in a supernatural manner. The Bible says His ways are not our ways, His ways are higher and they are great, they are supernatural. I want us to look at the following passage of scripture which is full of exciting supernatural activities.

For as the heavens are higher than the earth, so are my ways higher than your ways, and my thoughts than your thoughts. (Isaiah 55:9)

In the passage below there's a story involving four leprous men who were sitting at the entrance of the city gate.

And there were four leprous men at the entering in of the gate: and they said one to another, why sit we here until we die? (2 Kings 7:3)

City gates are strategic places; in the past that is where decisions and destinies for cities were settled; they are like our modern municipal town halls, where councilors and city leaders sit to decide on matters pertaining to the affairs of the city. As I said earlier on, God chooses our fights because we are not fighting for ourselves, God's battles are always referred to as the battle of the Lord. The four lepers represent a story of four men who found themselves in a place of isolation and desperation. They were left at the entrance of the city gates because they had leprosy, a disease that was contagious and as a result society did not allow them to be among those that were well. The history of leprosy goes back a long way, it is commonly known that those who were infected with this disease were quarantined from their communities due to the infectious nature of the disease. It was a standard procedure that such people should be quarantined in order to control the spread of the disease. It was during this time that these lepers made a profound decision.

Despite their location and their number, they made a profound faith decision. The supernatural aspect of warfare is always based on the faith factor; insignificant people at an insignificant place made an insignificant decision. It was unheard of that people with their condition would dare to enroll in an army, or, get into a fight against the military; in a proper camp with all food supplies. They were operating from a place of lack; they were outside the gates where they were dumped and left to die; yet somehow, they had faith to believe. They employed their faith and launched their supernatural attack with these words; "if we die we die; if we live we live"; that is a statement of risk.

This statement is familiar to most of the people who operate in faith. We have seen this statement before when the four Jewish boys in Babylon were faced with a similar situation; being a minority they said to the king if we live; we live; if die we die. Great results come out of these kinds of decisions. Supernatural warfare is not for the timid, it is for those that dare to go all the way; it's a sacrificial move that may even threaten one's life. In the natural it can be dubbed foolishness; in the spirit world it's what produces the manifestation of the supernatural; it's like a person having a third eye; seeing things that other people cannot see; like having information of the victory that was established in heaven by God and bringing it down to the natural world. In the case of the lepers, they were taking a move as if they overheard God's prophet when he said God intended to provide food supernaturally to a nation that was suffering from a drought that had reached alarming stages. When the lepers made the move; little did they know that the food supply was actually in the camp of the army that was camped not very far from where they were. There was a camp full of food; one had to tap into the mind of God to know where the food was; fortunately, they were the ones that responded and took a supernatural move; to their amazement, God came through for them; and this is how

God came through for them. With God minority is majority; where there is a will God makes a way; they were willing and God made a way. Upon arriving; the camp was ready for their plunder; when they took the first step God did the rest.

For the Lord had made the host of the Syrians to hear a noise of chariots, and a noise of horses, even the noise of a great host: and they said one to another, Lo, the king of Israel hath hired against us the kings of the Hittites, and the kings of the Egyptians, to come upon us. (2 Kings 7:6)

The above scripture is self-explaining; that the Syrians interpreted what took place that day as the king of Israel had come into an allied force with the Hittites and Egyptians to come and fight them. Yet in reality it was nothing but four lepers; this is a picture of heaven invading the natural realm in a supernatural way.

This situation of leprous men may look natural but on the other hand, if we were to measure the extent of what was transpiring one might want to conclude that even their leprosy was somehow connected to a spiritual condition of their nation. It was during this time that God spoke through a prophet that change was coming on a specific day, however, the message was not received positively. The response from the audience that this was intended for, was not positive. God's word must be received by faith without faith it is impossible to please God, even if people don't receive what God says, God's word still comes to pass with or without the participation of those that it was designed to benefit.

Faith requires risk; faith is like dying; in the book of Revelation, the Bible

says, 'they love not their lives unto the end'.
The four lepers were insignificant people who received a spiritual strategy that went ahead of them to weaken the enemy. Before they even arrived victory was in the bag. They walked into a prepared victory, spiritual warfare is about God fighting for you. Spiritual warfare is about battles that God fights using the method of lessor versus greater.

Here is a unique story of four men who were seated at a place of isolation and desperation, they were left there to die, they had a condition that would kill them slowly. Leprosy is a deadly disease that eats up parts of your body causing it to fall away until you eventually die.
In the case of these four lepers they found themselves in a difficult position, their country was in a state of famine that means in spite of their sickness there was no food for them. They faced a double jeopardy, not having food and sick at the same time.
However, when we consider the story as it unfolds, God had other plans in play for these men. They through their rejection were placed at a strategic place at the entrance of the city gates.
The position where the four lepers were seated, was not a place where anyone expected anything to come out of them. There are situations in the natural that do not seem promising, however spiritual laws and natural laws have different dynamics. Spiritual warfare looks beyond natural circumstances, it engages its strategies from a spiritual realm, not from a natural point of view.

It takes faith to activate the word of God. It took four sick people who were insignificant, who were sitting in an insignificant place. God sometimes uses insignificant people to bring significant results. Due to their desperation, they came to a decision that agreed with the plans of God in heaven. They decided to go to the camp of the enemy as their problem was not going to be resolved by going to their own camp. The lepers were excluded from their communities and if they went back to their communities they were not going to be received and there was no food. They decided to go to a camp where their enemy was camping, and the move seemed to please heaven, starting a turnaround.

Allow me to say that they engaged in spiritual warfare or they engaged in a spiritual warfare mode and from that moment on everything changed. In turn, they became national heroes, by the time this warfare was done they had gotten back their status as normal citizens. Spiritual warfare gives you validation to be accepted where you were not accepted before, and those that used to overlook you will overlook you no more. It is not a matter of what you look like, it's what you offer. They had a solution to a national crisis, they had discovered food in abundance as they went to that camp God made them sound like it was a mighty army coming against the camp of the enemy. Those that were in the enemy's camp ran away and left huge reserves of food and wealth. Arriving at the camp they discovered that it was empty.

When God is on your side, He amplifies your ability, what you cannot do alone He increases your ability, this is a true case of divine intervention, this was a supernatural intervention of heavens invading in the affairs of mankind on earth.

Four people brought the victory that was prophesied by a prophet that there was going to be food in the city in spite of their doubt and the voices of the gainsayers and the nay-sayers. God's word came to pass.

Then Elisha said, Hear ye the word of the LORD; Thus saith the LORD, To morrow about this time shall a measure of fine flour be sold for a shekel, and two measures of barley for a shekel, in the gate of Samaria.
(2 Kings 7:1)

REFLECTION AND PRAYER ACTIVATION

1. What did the enemy come to ______________do? The enemy ______________ to steal, kill and to destroy: I came that they might have life, and that they might have it more abundantly.

2. Spiritual warfare is likened to the wind. The wind blows where it wishes and you hear it's sound ______________ so it is with everyone who is born of the Spirit.

3. What does the bible say we wrestle with in the spiritual warfare? For we wrestle not against _________________ but against principalities ___________________ powers ______________ darkness of this world _______________ in high places.
4. What did Paul say he fought with at Ephesus that he likened to spiritual warfare? If after the manner of man, I fought with ____________at Ephesus _______________ let us eat and drink, for tomorrow we die.

5. What are our spiritual weapons? For our weapons of our warfare are not _________________ God to the pulling down of strong holds ______________ to the obedience of Christ.

6. Who smote the people who were at the door with blindness? ______________________.

7. Were angels involved in the release of Peter from prison? _________________________.
8. Who was involved in fighting the Assyrians and killed hundred fourscore and five thousand? _____________________.

9. What did God say about the size of Gideon's army?

10. Who did Joshua encounter and was told he was the captain of the heavenly armies? ______________________.

11. What did David say when he faced the giant? Who did he say would give the giant into his hands? ______________________.

12. Who made the Syrians hear noises of chariots, horses and great host when the four lepers were approaching the camp of the Syrians

1. John 10:10 [KJV]
2. John 3: 8 [AMP]
3. Ephesians 6:12 [KJV]
4. 1 Corinthians 15: 32[KJV]
5. 2 Corinthians 10:4 [KJV]
6. Genesis 19:11 [KVJ]
7. Acts 12:7 [KJV]
8. 2 Kings 19:35 [KVJ]
9. Judges 7:2 [KVJ]
10. Joshua 5:15 [KJV]
11. 1 Samuel 17:45 [KJV]
12. 2 Kings 7:6 [KJV]

PRAYER

Lord fill me with abundant life, I want to be a spirit led believer who understands how to warfare and bring down principalities in high places. Give me understanding to discern representatives of darkness so that I may live a life full of eternal blessings, understanding how to use the spiritual weapons that are available for me to bring those that are walking in disobedience to the obedience of Christ. Release your angels to fight on my behalf just like you did for the lepers and Peter and all the saints because you are the captain of the heavenly armies. I want to be a giant slayer like David. Amen.

CHAPTER 5

SUPERNATURAL WORSHIP

God created man for fellowship and worship, these two work hand in hand, worship is a lifestyle of all Gods children. This is evident from the very first book of the Bible, where in the cool of the day God came to commune with Adam in the garden of Eden continuously.

And they heard the voice of the LORD God walking in the garden in the cool of the day: and Adam and his wife hid themselves from the presence of the LORD God amongst the trees of the garden. (Genesis 3:8)

Eden means "the presence of God". This is where Adam and God fellowshipped. God had lost His worship leader in heaven Satan or Lucifer as he was known. His primary duties in heaven was to lead worship until the day he was expelled and cast out from heaven to earth after iniquity was found in him. It is then when God decided to create man to replace him for he had lost His worshipper.

How art thou fallen from heaven, O Lucifer, son of the morning! how art thou cut down to the ground, which didst weaken the nations (Isaiah 14:12)

Lucifer was perfect in all of his ways, in charge of worship in heaven until iniquity was found in him.

Thou wast perfect in thy ways from the day that thou wast created, till iniquity was found in thee. (Ezekiel 28:15)

The word iniquity according to the Webster dictionary means; absence of, or deviation from, just dealing; want of rectitude or uprightness; gross injustice; unrighteousness; wickedness. Lucifer therefore was separated from God because of bad motives and wickedness that was found in him. Iniquity separates mankind from God, so true worship can not be mingled with a heart that has iniquity as seen in the book of Isaiah.

But your iniquities have separated between you and your God, and your sins have hid his face from you, that he will not hear. (Isaiah 59:2)

Lucifer's expullsion from heaven was due to his iniquities, he lost his position of worship and man was created in his place to be God's true worshiper.

Therefore, man took the position of worshiping God just as Lucifer was in heaven, man was raised because God had lost His first son, Lucifer. Adam was not the first son of God to fall into sin Lucifer was.
He fell from his position as a worshiper and became the fallen angel, angels are referred to as sons of God. He wanted someone who would take that place of worship; as we see evidenced by His creating man in His own image for worship. It is important to note that man was created for the presence of God. Therefore, worship creates an environment which God lives in. God and worship are inseparable it is only through worship that an environment of the presence of God is created. When Adam sinned against God he could not continue to be in the presence of God, he went and hid himself among the trees, as seen in the above scripture. The purpose of sin is to remove one from the presence of God just as the wages of sin is death. The word death means separation when sin is present the presence of God is absent, ultimately Adam was expelled from the garden because wherever there is sin God will not have fellowship with anyone.

THE PSALMIST AND THE LIFTING OF HANDS

O come, let us worship and bow down: let us kneel before the LORD our maker. (Psalms 95:6)

The Psalmist was referring to one of the postures of worship which is to bow down. Bowing down to the One who created us, to the One who made the heavens and the earth, is a sign of honor and reverence. The Psalmist understood that very well, hence, he made the statement and said "Let us" as if he was inviting all of God's creation to join him in worship. Worship has a lot to do with posture. For example; in some cultures, especially in Africa, it is a requirement that when one is addressing honorable people, he should take a posture of kneeling down as a sign of respect. I recall when I was in Lagos Nigeria, I'd meet people in the lobby of the hotel I was staying in who had come to realize that I was a visiting preacher and they would prostrate before me. It is part of their culture. It felt strange at first but later, I had to accept it because they did that in honor and respect.

Worship makes you one with the One that you worship. The moment you begin to reverence God, you come into the realm of the presence of God and you begin to experience all that is His. God is the Lord God of Hosts, which means He is the God of the armies of heaven. God never loses any of his battles; so are they that worship Him. Knowing the God that you worship is to become victorious, it's a supernatural posture that one gets into that enables you to become a member of the armies of heaven. Spiritual warfare involves postures, as the Psalmist stated in the above scripture that 'bowing down' is one of them. In the scripture below, Aaron the High Priest had this to say:

AARON AND THE LIFTING OF HANDS

And Aaron lifted up his hand toward the people, and blessed them, and came down from offering of the sin offering, and the burnt offering, and peace offerings. (Leviticus 9:22)

In the Old Testament setting, we are seeing another posture from a representative of God, Aaron the High Priest. He lifted his hands and blessed the people during the time of burnt offering. The work of the priest in the Old Testament was to be the mediator between God and man. So, we see him here using the practice of lifting hands as he blesses the people. That is another posture of worship.

There are many scriptures that speak about the lifting of hands and it is important to note that in worship 'bowing down' and the 'lifting of hands' is a sign of spiritual warfare. It may not look significant in the natural but in the spiritual realm, when hands are lifted there is a lot of spiritual activity taking place. Satan and his kingdom get weakened when the saints of God take postures of reverence to God. Kneeling before God, the lifting of hands before God is more than just a posture, it is an inward expression that is followed up by an outward expression. Even lying prostrate before God speaks of total surrender, it is an expression of love to the One who made us and in turn releases blessings, hence, the Priest used lifting of hands as he blessed the people.

KING SOLOMON AND THE LIFTING OF HANDS

> And it was so, that when Solomon had made an end of praying all this *prayer and supplication unto the LORD, he arose from before the altar of the LORD, from kneeling on his knees with his hands spread up to heaven.*
> *(1 Kings 8:54)*

King Solomon understood the principle and he also lifted his hands, bowed down before God. The scripture below speaks of a corporate worship as people came into agreement as they worshipped God with their faces to the ground.

EZRA AND THE LIFTING OF HANDS

And Ezra blessed the LORD, the great God. And all the people answered, Amen, Amen, with lifting up their hands: and they bowed their heads, and worshipped the LORD with their faces to the ground.
(Nehemiah 8:6)

This is a beautiful picture of what corporate worship is, it is to bless God, it is to acknowledge that it is through Him we live and have our beings, that He deserves the highest worship. The Psalmist had this to say:

So I will bless you as long as I live, I will lift my hands in your name.
(Psalms 63:4)

Lift up your hands to the sanctuary and bless the Lord. (Psalms 134:2)

When we lift our hands to the Lord and bless God, something supernatural begins to take place in the natural. If we were facing resistance from Satan and any challenges in any area in our lives God surely renders the heavens and intervenes on our behalf. Our postures of worship must never be overlooked.

MOSES AND THE LIFTING OF HANDS

Moses demonstrated a posture of worship during the time of the battle between the Amalekites and the children of Israel. This posture, if one was to look at it in the natural, it may not make sense at all. In order to appreciate what Moses was doing, we have to take it back to what God had said earlier on in reference to the Amalekites. The Amalekites were nothing but a stumbling block to the mission of the people of God. They with stood Moses and prevented the people of Israel from forging ahead to the promised land. This may again look like it was a natural distraction, however, Israel represented the blessings of God that was going to come through their lineage. This was a spiritual assignment from God through the chosen race. Therefore, whosoever stood against them was indirectly stopping spiritual blessings that were going to benefit the whole world. And God in response said this in the following scripture.

For he said, Because the LORD hath sworn that the LORD will have war with Amalek from generation to generation." (Exodus 17:16)

Amalekites became Gods prime enemy as God alluded to Moses, He was going to make war with them from generation to generation. So, there was a battle line drawn in the spiritual realm by God against the Amalekites. It took Moses to tap into the realm of the spirit on how to conduct the spiritual warfare against the Amalekites. He then took a posture that was unique as he went to the hill with some of his leaders to conduct a spiritual warfare by way of the lifting of hands as the scripture below:

And Moses said unto Joshua, Choose us out men, and go out, fight with Amalek: tomorrow I will stand on the top of the hill with the rod of God in mine hand. So Joshua did as Moses had said to him, and fought with Amalek: and Moses, Aaron, and Hur went up to the top of the hill. And it came to pass, when Moses held up his hand, that Israel prevailed: and when he let down his hand, Amalek prevailed. (Exodus 17:9-11)

We see how the lifting of the hands produced supernatural results that whenever he lifted his hands Joshua prevailed against the Amalekites. This speaks of what happens when conducting spiritual warfare there's supernatural transmission of the presence of God that defuses the enemy and stops him in a way that cannot be explained in the natural. Paul the Apostle, in the New Testament had this to say in the scripture below:

I will therefore that men pray everywhere, lifting up holy hands, without wrath and doubting. (1Timothy 2:8)

What the Apostle was saying, when men are lifting up holy hands in prayer there is a spiritual dimension that gets accomplished. This is a spiritual activity that results in a physical manifestation. King David in the following psalm, a man who understood spiritual warfare portrayed in the following words:

A Psalm of David. Blessed be the LORD my strength, which teacheth my hands to war, and my fingers to fight: (Psalm 144:1)

David said the Lord trains our hands for war. The lifting up of hands of all the children of God during the time of worship is a sign of spiritual warfare. That's the picture that is revealed when Moses lifted up his hands during the time Joshua was fighting with the Amalekites, every time Moses lift up his hand Joshua was having the upper hand, and every time Moses' hands were down Joshua was losing. Our victories begin in the spiritual realm before they manifest in the natural. The natural takes its tone from the spiritual. The position of Moses on the hill and his lifting up of hands represented a spiritual authority of one who is worshipping, to bring down that which has already happened in heaven so that it be manifested on earth.

TRUE WORSHIPPERS

Jesus revealed to the woman in Samaria that the hour had come for true worshipers. His emphasis was that they will worship the Father in spirit and in truth for God seeks such. Jesus was addressing a misconception which existed between the Samaritans and the Jewish people. There was disagreement over where people should worship, on which mountain they ought to worship. Jesus began to reveal that worship has little to do with the geographic setting, it is more of a spiritual posture than a physical one. And he alluded to the fact that now true worshipers will need not to seek places of worship, but will connect with God spiritually and supernaturally.

God is a Spirit: and they that worship him must worship him in spirit and in truth. (John 4:24)

Worship releases the purposes of God on the earth. God's intention on earth is to have worshippers, and true worshippers are not found in religious settings, or in temples made by man's hands. It is their spiritual relationship with God, their intimate relationship with God that makes them worshipers. God is seeking those with a heart that is true, that is willing to worship Him and if He finds such He manifests himself on the earth. He said this about David, "I have found a man after my own heart". David was a worshipper and that is what made him a good warrior. Warriors and worship are twins.

But now thy kingdom shall not continue: the Lord hath sought him a man after his own heart, and the Lord hath commanded him to be captain over his people, because thou hast not kept that which the Lord commanded thee. (1 Samuel 13:14)

It is interesting to note that David's captaincy was triggered by a fact that God said "I've found a man after my own heart".
First and foremost, the heart of David wanted to worship God. God is a warrior, who fights against the forces of evil, and His worshippers are the same, they want to uproot evil and establish the Will and purposes of God. Saul was fired and David was hired. Deception, iniquity, half commitments and compromises have no place in the heart of a worshipper.

Lucifer was fired and God is seeking those He can hire, who can worship Him in spirit and in truth.

ABRAHAM THE WORSHIPPER

God told Abraham to go on a three-day journey to a place where he was going to worship Him. Upon arriving at a place, he told his young men to stay behind, while he and his son went to worship as seen in the scripture below.

And Abraham said unto his young men, Abide ye here with the ass; and I and the lad will go yonder and worship, and come again to you.
(Genesis 22:5)

Worship demands separation as I said earlier. It makes you one with the One you worship, it's an intimate thing where you respond heart to heart. It was a personal encounter that brought him to the place of worship. To worship God, you don't want to follow what or how other people are feeling, it is important that you take along with you those that see the same things that you see and value the same things that you value. Abraham went with his son and left his young men behind. On the mountain of Moriah, Abraham experienced a supernatural encounter with God. God revealed to him another dimension of Himself. It is at this mountain that Abraham said the name of God is Jehovah Jireh. Worship allows you to break through and get into the place of provision. Worship reveals God's treasures and He only reveals this to true worshipers.
When He finds true worshipers, He manifests Himself. Worship is super-

natural and it triggers the agenda of heaven and activates the purposes of God in the earth. Abraham was confirmed by God to be His friend during a time of worship. He went to Mount Moriah to worship and he told his servants to remain behind while he took his son Isaac up to the place of worship. Worship requires separation, hence, God seeks true worshippers and they are those He finds. They worship Him spiritually, they worship Him truthfully, when He finds them. The supernatural connection releases the heavens on earth.

Worship is the only activity in heaven. God dwells in the realm of Worship. Worship is intimate. Abraham experienced God's provision at the place of Worship, it is in that place where he called Him Jehovah Jireh, God who provides, worship reveals God's attributes, one gets to know him even by name. A ram was provided at a place of worship, hence the book of John emphasizes that God seeks true worshipper.

JEHOSHAPHAT THE WORSHIP WARRIOR

Jehoshaphat was the king who employed a spiritual warfare strategy that worked supernatural results without the use of force or sword or an armor.

And Jehoshaphat bowed his head with his face to the ground: and all Judah and the inhabitants of Jerusalem fell before the Lord, worshipping the Lord. (2 Chronicles 20:18)

Jehoshaphat was facing a difficult time, he consulted God in prayer. After praying, he employed a spiritual strategy that was unique. His strategy confirms that you don't need a huge military or much physical stamina if you have a spiritual strategy. You can gain victory if God is on your side, and if you have faith in Him and are in tune with His heart. If only you can be true to yourself, God can be true to you to establish you as a prince. True worship begins with true connection with God's heart. He prayed to God sincerely, committed everything to God wholeheartedly.

And said, O Lord God of our fathers, art not thou God in heaven? and rulest not thou over all the kingdoms of the heathen? and in thine hand is there not power and might, so that none is able to withstand thee? Art, not thou our God, who didst drive out the inhabitants of this land before thy people Israel, and gavest it to the seed of Abraham thy friend for ever?And they dwelt therein, and have built thee a sanctuary therein for thy name, saying, If, when evil cometh upon us, as the sword, judgment, or pestilence, or famine, we stand before this house, and in thy presence, (for thy name is in this house,) and cry unto thee in our affliction, then thou wilt hear and help. And now, behold, the children of Ammon and Moab and mount Seir, whom thou wouldest not let Israel invade, when they came out of the land of Egypt, but they turned from them, and destroyed them not;Behold, I say, how they reward us, to come to cast us out of thy possession, which thou hast given us to inherit.O our God, wilt thou not judge them? for we have no might against this great company that cometh against us; neither know we what to do: but our eyes are upon thee. And all Judah stood before the Lord, with their little ones, their wives, and their children." (2 Chronicles 20:6- 12)

God responded prophetically. God does nothing unless He reveals it to His servants the prophets. Gods prophetic word releases faith, because true faith comes through hearing the word of God. The sure word of prophecy is the basis of true faith that produces the supernatural. The wages of sin is death, sin produces fear, ultimately death.

And he said, Hearken ye, all Judah, and ye inhabitants of Jerusalem, and thou king Jehoshaphat, Thus saith the Lord unto you, Be not afraid nor dismayed by reason of this great multitude; for the battle is not yours, but God's. (2 Chronicles 20:18)

King Jehoshaphat responded with a worship mode. Worship is a celebration mode that accelerates the supernatural. As seen in the scripture he began to worship God and the rest was the supernatural manifestation of the victory of the day.

Jehoshaphat was in a difficult predicament, so he consulted God about his situation. This is one of the classic spiritual worship strategies that the bible has ever revealed. I would like to say, in my view he used a three-fold approach; he prayed, received a prophecy and he worshipped then God brought the victory. Supernatural worship involves these three segments.

Prayer does not exclude worship, and prophecy does not exclude worship. These three are equally important. When Jehoshaphat inquired of God he got God to respond, then he took the next level of positioning himself to see God's intervention; he did this through worshipping God.

He did not physically engage the three armies he was fighting against having been told by God that the battle was not his. Spiritual warfare acknowledges who is fighting on our behalf, even though it is physical the battle is the Lord's. God has never lost a battle, He has won all His fights, so all we need to do is worship Him. As we worship the host of heaven is dispatched to wage warfare against our enemies who may seem natural, but are spiritually controlled. Worship connects us with the spiritual realm, which is the realm which all our physical challenges are realized. Jehoshaphat understood that principle, and as he executed it he experienced a tremendous breakthrough.

Spiritual warfare has similar results, that something supernatural happens to the opposition without the involvement of human effort. It is God fighting on our behalf in response to what we said in prayer in agreement. Without realizing it, worshipping God is the acknowledgement, or thanking God in advance that it is done, even before we could see it. Jehoshaphat went into a celebration mode because God promised, therefore, he was celebrating the promises of God. It was when he began to worship that the enemy began to kill one another.
When heaven intervenes, our enemies become self-destructive and begin to defeat themselves. He is a loving caring God.

And Jehoshaphat bowed his head with his face to the ground: and all Judah and the inhabitants of Jerusalem fell before the LORD, worshipping the LORD. And the Levites, of the children of the Kohathites, and of the children of the Korhites, stood up to praise the LORD God of Israel with a loud voice on high. And they rose early in the morning, and went forth into the wilderness of Tekoa: and as they went forth, Jehoshaphat stood and said, Hear me, O Judah, and ye inhabitants of Jerusalem; Believe in the LORD your God, so shall ye be established; believe his prophets, so shall ye prosper. And when he had consulted with the people, he appointed singers unto the LORD, and that should praise the beauty of holiness, as they went out before the army, and to say, Praise the LORD; for his mer- cy endureth for ever. And when they began to sing and to praise, the LORD set ambushments against the children of Ammon, Moab, and mount Seir, which were come against Judah; and they were smitten. For the children of Ammon and Moab stood up against the inhabitants of mount Seir, utterly to slay and destroy them: and when they had made an end of the inhabitants of Seir, every one helped to destroy another."

(2 Chronicles 20:18 -23)

REFLECTION AND PRAYER ACTIVATION

1. What was the main purpose of God creating man? For ________________ and ___________________.

2. How does God want us to worship Him? God is Spirit and they that____________ Him must ____________ Him in spirit and in_________________.

3. What happened to Joshua when Moses lifted his hands? Moses, Aaron, and Hur went up to the top of the hill. And it came to pass, when Moses held up his hand, ____________ prevailed: and when he let down his hand, ______________ prevailed.

4. Lifting up of hands before God is for worshiping him. As well as? I will therefore that men ____________ everywhere, lifting up holy hands, without___________ and ______________.

5. Why did Abraham go to the mountain with Isaac? And Abraham said unto his young men, Abide ye here with the ass; and I and the lad will go _________________ and ______________ , and come again to you

6. What did Jehoshaphat do? And Jehoshaphat ______________ his head with his face to the ground: and all Judah and the inhabitants of Jerusalem fell before the Lord, ____________________ the Lord.

1. John 4:24 [KJV]
2. Exodus 17:9-11 [KJV]

3. Genesis 22:5 [KJV]
4. 2 Chronicles 20:18 [KJV]

PRAYER

Lord I want to worship You in spirit and in truth and to be in true fellowship and true worship in your presence. Make me to have clean hands and a heart that is not defiled with iniquity, may I live a life of total separation that comes to you and bows to you and worshipping only you, to you only will I bow down continuously in Jesus name. I lift my hands up to Your Name and thank You for your grace and your victory.
I ask for victory in the following situations:
Amen.

CHAPTER 6

SUPERNATURAL HUMILITY

The Bible is full of heroes of faith; most of them obtained great testimonies of their walk of faith; primarily due to the way they carried themselves and the way they presented the gospel. In humility of heart; they portrayed a style which is worth imitating. This is seen throughout the early church ministry; people such as Paul the Apostle who was one of the founding fathers of the Christian faith. We find this in one of his writings:

Serving the Lord with all humility of mind, and with many tears, and temptations, which befell me by the lying-in wait of the Jews (Acts 20:19)

This is just a glimpse of what it takes to carry out the work of God in such conditions as we see being portrayed. Unless one is humble enough he cannot endure the many challenges that are attached to the preaching of the gospel. Hence Paul refers to serving the Lord with humility of heart. The word humility from the Webster dictionary means

1."The state or quality of being humble; freedom from pride and arro-;gance; lowliness of mind; a modest estimate of one's worth; a sense of one's own unworthiness through imperfection and sinfulness; self-abasement; humbleness."

2. "An act of submission in courtesy."
The word humility for the lack of words to fully explain it; one might just say it carries a magic formula. Humility can cause one to access lesser judgement even before the courts of law. It has such diplomacy and grace that can cause one to obtain advocacy, even when he deserved a severe punishment for the wrong that he might have caused. The word 'humility' appears in the entire Bible fifty-six (56) times, particularly in the King James version, and it deals with the number of issues. A further study on humility shows us that Jesus is a model of humility as seen throughout his life.

And being found in fashion as a man, he humbled himself, and became obedient unto death, even the death of the cross. (Philippians 2:8)

The death of our Lord Jesus Christ on the cross is one of the purest examples of humility, of divinity becoming humanity, as an act of humility. Jesus' death on the cross is referred to, as an act of humbling Himself, He agreed to die a low-level death, a death of a criminal, when He Himself had committed no crime.

He died as a sinner when He had committed no sin. It was an act of humility. He came to save those that were dying in their sins. In order to do that He became human and demonstrated humility by the life he lived and ultimately by the way He died. In one incident He washed the feet of His disciples, to explain that gesture He said:

If I then, your Lord and Master, have washed your feet; ye also ought to wash one another's feet. (John 13:12)

But he that is greatest among you shall be your servant. (Matthew 23:11)

He said, "He who wants to be the greatest among you must be the servant of all." Jesus is the greatest servant that ever lived. To be the greatest you must exercise humility. Humility is the key to greatness, just by looking at the scripture we can see it establishes supernaturalism, although to reason it naturally will not make sense. One might be asking the question, how can God become a man? It defies human logic and reasoning unless one begins to view it as a supernatural act, only then can it make sense. So allow me to say humility is supernatural. We live in the world that is full of competition; the human race puts a high value on people based on their social status. There is an upper class and the lower class; the golden rule scenario; that speaks of he who has much gold; let him rule. There are constant wars that are fought over who is the greatest and who is the weakest; nations compete for the number one position. I have travelled to a number of countries; one thing is common to every country I visited; there is always a highlight of why they think that particular country is greater than the others. Sometimes they do that through comparison of their national heroes or what they have accomplished throughout their history. It takes humility to acknowledge that there is no greatness outside God. It was humility that made Jesus the greatest. There was a particular incident where Jesus was told that He was good, and He denied it. This shows how much humility was in his heart as seen in the scripture below:

And Jesus said unto him, Why callest thou me good? none is good, save one, that is, God. (Luke 18:19)

That alone is the statement of faith. I have been observing what has happened in church history. Many great movements started and when they shifted the focus to men that movement collapsed. When God is excluded disaster is inevitable. Paul the Apostle said these humbling words:

But I keep under my body, and bring it into subjection: lest that by any means when I have preached to others, I myself should be a cast away. (1Corinthians 9:27)

Humility is a virtue, it's God given and it comes out of the heart that seeks to honour God; however many have lost their place and lost the grace of God because of their lack of humility. The opposite of humility, or, grace is pride. Lucifer, once a powerful worshiper did not carry himself in humility; he was cast out of heaven. Many have become outcast by self-imposition; the psalmist had this to say in reference to humility:

The sacrifices of God are a broken spirit: a broken and a contrite heart, O God, thou wilt not despise. (Psalms 51:17)

According to Webster dictionary, the word 'contrite' is: "Broken down with grief and penitence; deeply sorrowful for sin because it is displeasing to God; humbly and thoroughly penitent".

It takes a heart that is touched by God to release such qualities. As I said Lucifer lost his position when he operated outside humility. When one tries to raise himself above God; that's pride. In the New Testament there is a story about King Herod who was eaten up by worms; because he thought himself to be above God.

And immediately the angel of the Lord smote him because he gave not God the glory: and he was eaten of worms, and gave up the ghost. (Acts 12:23)

When people don't acknowledge God because of the pride of their heart; such things take place in their lives; King Herod was smitten and died. There are so many references in the Bible; in the book of Esther, there is a decorated story of Mordecai versus Haman.

And Haman told Zeresh his wife and all his friends everything that had befallen him. Then said his wise men and Zeresh his wife unto him, If Mordecai be of the seed of the Jews, before whom thou hast begun to fall, thou shalt not prevail against him, but shalt surely fall before him. (Esther 6:13)

Haman was full of pride and he began to conspire against Mordecai. Mordecai was a man of God with humility of heart as seen in the way he raised Esther as his daughter; she knew how to fast and pray. The scripture speaks of what happens to proud people if they come against those that are connected to God and humbly serve him. The life of Haman ends in tragedy just as his wife predicted.

So they hanged Haman on the gallows that he had prepared for Mordecai. Then was the king's wrath pacified. (Esther 7:10)

Humility produces supernatural outcomes; those that walk in humility will have supernatural results following them. Jesus humbled Himself to show us He was the humility of God personified; His name 'Emmanuel' speaks of 'God with us'. For God to become a man is a picture of humility; it denotes the supernatural; it's unnatural for God to be a man. Jesus appeared irrelevant, but He was relevant all the time; He looked like He was backward and outdated. Why would God become a man? But through all that He did, He was ahead all the time; God works in reverse.

Jesus humbled Himself as the Bible says "unto the death of a cross". Humility might look like invisibility, but on the contrary, it is visibility in reverse. The reverse is a backward motion, not an accidental movement. This is the way to look at it, not in a negative sense or a negative motion; it is a deliberate considered action. One can be reminded of when driving a car and you reach the desired destiny; you park the car in the parking lot which sometimes requires you to reverse into a place where you are going to secure the car. This is for safety and getting you ready to take off; it is a place where it gets you ready to go. As I have said there is a reverse manoeuvre to get you to that place.

The reverse motion, therefore, may be viewed as primarily a place of preparation to take off to a higher dimension or to a place ahead. It is a getting ready to go higher to a more visible and valid place in life. John the baptist in the scripture below said these powerful words:

He must increase, but I must decrease (John 3:30)

HUMILITY IS A KINGDOM OF GOD REVELATION

Humility is a decision, not an imposition; to decrease is a voluntary submission. However, humility does not make one disappear, rather it's a decrease to appear or to be elevated. Humility and elevation work hand in hand; the psalmist understood this principle very well.

For promotion cometh neither from the east, nor from the west, nor from the south. But God is the judge: he putteth down one, and setteth up another. (Psalm 75:6 -7)

Understanding that promotion does not come from the east or the west, but promotion comes from above is helpful to being humble. There is no value in adopting different cultural values to achieve promotion in life. I am all for promoting goods with such slogans as 'Proudly South African', but not people. Promotion comes from Jesus when one humbles himself before the Lord. We thank God for the West; thank God for the other nations of the world, but all nations are blessed when God is their God and they serve Him with humility in their hearts; they can flourish in the blessings of heaven regardless of their geographic location or cultural background; east, west or south, it does not matter. Humility is what brings the blessings of God.

Humility is a twin brother of servanthood as seen in the life of Moses, the servant of the Lord. Moses was chosen by God and what is interesting about his life was that he was one of those people God chose as a leader from a humble background. His job description at the time of his calling speaks volumes as he was looking after the flock of his father-in law. God got him into the position of leadership by His election of grace, while he was busy looking after the flock of his father in-law (Jethro).

God has a tendency of picking up those that are busy serving in humble positions and calls them into His service. We see later in Moses' life as he was humbled by what he saw God doing through him that he realized it took God's grace for him to come into the service of the Lord. This produced a level of humility in him that prompted him to make the following statement.

And he said unto him, if thy presence goes not with me, carry us not up hence. (Exodus 33:15)

In the past Moses was known for going where he wanted to go, executing what he wanted to execute, and now he had changed. He was now a graduate of his past mistakes, and he came to acknowledge his total reliance on God through humility. This is confirmed by the words he said, "We cannot go unless your Presence carries us". These are the words of a man who had come to the realization that the working of the supernatural God was involved in his life. His heart was full of humility and through life experience, he knew he can only advance when God is taking the lead.

THE CHILDREN OF ISSACHAR AS EXAMPLES OF HUMILITY

And of the children of Issachar, which were men that had understanding of the times, to know what Israel ought to do; the heads of them were two hundred, and all their brethren were at their commandment.
(1 Chronicles 12:32)

To lead is servanthood and good leaders understand humility. I'd like to believe that the children of Issachar were exemplary and that's what made them leaders among their brethren. Here is an interesting scripture in the bible that described the children of Issachar as donkeys that couch between two burdens, which simply means a humble animal, a burden bearer symbolizing servanthood.

Issachar is a strong ass couching down between two burdens
(Genesis 49:14)

Donkeys are known for their service to mankind; they are very humble creatures that are hard working, and they can be easily described as servants. That is why the children of Issachar are referred to as 'Donkeys'. They played a pivotal role in the community as they provided supernatural insight, they operated in the supernatural word of knowledge for direction. The children of Israel in-order for them to get that information they needed to go among the children of Issachar. Leadership is a supernatural ability given to some of the members of the body of Christ to provide direction. When Jesus entered Jerusalem he was riding on a donkey, which again speaks of how donkeys are servants with humble tasks including taking people from here to there. Servants of God are like donkeys that carry the supernatural that Jesus had burdened them with, one of the characteristics of servants is that they don't appoint themselves but they are chosen by God. Paul was the servant of God by divine appointment.

DAVID A HUMBLE SERVANT SENT BY HIS FATHER

David was sent by his father to offer service during the time they were in the war. His humility made him go without asking questions, even though he knew this could or may trigger tension with his brothers. He was misunderstood by his brothers, who often mistook him for someone who came of his own accord. They overlooked the fact that he was sent by his father. Even though he was opposed by his brothers he did not look back as he took this as an assignment that was given to him by his father and he carried it out in humility with a servant spirit.

And Eliab his eldest brother heard when he spake unto the men, and Eli-

ab's anger was kindled against David, and he said, Why camest thou down hither? and with whom hast thou left those few sheep in the wilderness? I know thy pride, and the naughtiness of thine heart; for thou art come down that thou mightest see the battle. And David said, What have I now done? Is there not a cause? (1Samuel 17:28)

This type of humility in David's life was confirmed by God in words seen in the scripture below:

But now thy kingdom shall not continue: the LORD hath sought him a man after his own heart, and the LORD hath commanded him to be captain over his people because thou hast not kept that which the LORD commanded thee. (1 Samuel 13:14)

Humility does not respond to confrontation in the same spirit, rather it seeks to give in so that amicable resolves can be obtained. It takes the broken spirit of someone who does not believe in strife, but rather operates in humility to achieve this unity and peace.

The sacrifices of God are a broken spirit: a broken and a contrite heart, O God, thou wilt not despise. (Psalms 51:17)

REFLECTION AND PRAYER ACTIVATION

1. What did Paul serve the Lord in? Serving the Lord with all_________of mind, and with many _____________, and __________ , which befell me by the lying-in wait of the Jews

2. Jesus walked in humility. And being found in fashion as a man, He _________ , and became obedient unto death, even the death of the cross.

3. Jesus taught that if He Himself served as a symbol of humility saying, 'If I then, your Lord and Master, have ________your________ ; ye also ought to wash one another's feet'.

4. What are the greatest meant to do for others? But he that is greatest among you shall be your _______________.

5. How do you get promoted? For cometh neither from the east, nor from the west, nor from the south. But ___________is the judge: he putteth down one, and ___________ up another.

1. Acts 20:19 [KJV]
2. Philippians 2:8 [KJV]
3. John 13:12 [KJV]
4. Matthew 23:11 [KJV]
5. Psalms 75:6 -7 [KJV]

PRAYER

Lord give me the grace to serve you with humility of heart and the fear of the Lord to be just like you even though you were God, you humbled yourself and you became an example even through your sacrificial death. You washed your disciples feet and you demonstrated a true heart of a servant. May I not seek to be served but to serve because you resist the proud and you give grace to the simple, may I decrees that you may increase, thank you Jesus Amen.

CHAPTER 7

SUPERNATURAL PRAYER

In the kingdom of God prayers are absolutely essential, there is no supernatural activities that happens without the prayers that are offered by the saints. The saints are those whom God has given the responsibility to activate supernatural happenings, they bring heaven's agenda onto the earth through supernatural prayers. When the saints pray they deal with all aspects of life where there is sin they seek God's pardon, where there are offences one to another, prayer seeks to rectify that by way of confession and reflection so that there is nothing that can hinder God from moving because sin is capable of blocking the blessings of God from flowing.

Therefore, confess your sins to one another [your false steps, your offences, and pray for one another, that you may be healed and restored. The heartfelt and persistent prayer of a righteous man (believer) can accomplish much when put into action and made effective by God it is dynamic and can have tremendous power. (James 5:16 AMP)

James, the Apostle, explains why the prayers of the saints are important. He explains that through prayer saints get to bring about each other's healing which means they carry a healing grace. He started by mentioning that there is need to confess their sins one to another. It is through prayer that the saints detox and renounce bad habits and this causes their prayers to become unique and effective. The prayers of the saints carry a unique value, and God honours them. When they rise before the Father they carry a fragrance that causes heaven to move and they activate the blessings of God on the earth. James, the Apostle, explained that the righteous man's prayers accomplish much and release tremendous results. The role of a believer in the kingdom of God is ambassadorial, it is a channel through which heaven speaks. The Bible calls them the saints of the Lord, these are they that God has set apart to be used by God for the matters pertaining to earth. When they pray, heaven agrees with them and releases what they have requested, because they are in right standing with God. They have obtained a position of relationship with God through the sacrificial death of Jesus Christ on the cross.

He made Christ who knew no sin to [judicially] be sin on our behalf so that in Him we would become the righteousness of God [that is, we would be made acceptable to Him and placed in a right relationship with Him by His gracious loving kindness]. (2 Corinthians 5:21)

The believers have been given a sphere of influence, and therefore God responds to them and brings their desired requests through supernatural avenues. Throughout the Bible, there are so many incidents where God clearly invites the saints to come and meet with Him through prayer. He is always seeking for someone to approach Him, but He does not always find those who are willing to take up His invitation.

I searched for a man among them who would build up the wall and stand in the gap before Me for [the sake of] the land, that I would not destroy it, but I found no one [not even one] (Ezekiel 22:30)

In most cases, when God finds someone to stand in the gap on behalf of the land, He then releases His blessings and His grace through that someone. That is why it is important to respond to His invitation.

Call to Me and I will answer you, and tell you [and even show you] great and mighty things, [things which have been confined and hidden], which you do not know and understand and cannot distinguish. (Jeremiah 33:3)

It is clear from the scripture that God wants to show great things and mighty things to those that respond to His call to prayer. There is so much God has in His heart to give or to release to His children when they pray. The psalmist is in agreement with what God wants to do in response to prayer.

O thou that hearest prayer, unto thee, shall all flesh come (Psalm 65:2)

Our God is known for hearing and answering prayer as clearly indicated above, and all people can come to Him. There are so many gods that people subscribe to, however, there is only one and true God. One of his names is 'Yahweh' the covenant loving God who hears and answers prayers. He values the prayers of His children, as He says in His own words; 'Call and I will answer you,' as a Father He delights in coming through for His children. Jesus the Son of the living God was a role model when it comes to praying for the saints.

....made intercession for the transgressors. (Isaiah 53:12)

The last portion of the scripture speaks of the role of Jesus as an intercessor, a role He still holds, even today, at the right hand of the throne of His Father, always praying for the saints. The scripture below clearly instructs that we should consider Jesus who played the role of mediation. The Old Testament priests spiritual work included praying and offering sacrifices.

Wherefore, holy brethren, partakers of the heavenly calling, consider the Apostle and High Priest of our profession, Christ Jesus (Hebrews 3:1)

A PRECIOUS PLACE FOR PRAYER IN HEAVEN

In the book of Revelation, prayers have a special place where they are stored in heaven, and that place is in golden vials that are before the altar of God as seen in the scripture below:

And when he had taken the book, the four beasts and four and twenty elders fell down before the Lamb, having every one of them harps, and golden vials full of odours, which are the prayers of saints. (Revelation 5:8)

The prayers of the saints are kept in a golden vial and they have a fragrance of incense that is released before the Throne of God. When saints are praying it is precious before God and He responds and acts supernaturally. Allow me to say at this point prayers are not just mere words, empty statements, they carry a certain value that can change and shape history. Nations are preserved, families are protected, disasters and accidents are averted. The prayers of the saints are supernatural and they can stop, or, change situations that were designed to be catastrophic.

And another angel came and stood at the altar, having a golden censer; and there was given unto him much incense, that he should offer it with prayers of all saints upon the golden altar which was before the throne. And the smoke of the incense, which came with the prayers of the saints, ascended up before God out of the angel's hand.

And the angel took the censer and filled it with fire of the altar, and cast it into the earth: and there were voices, and thunderings, and lightning, and an earthquake. (Revelation 8:35)

As mentioned in the scriptures, the golden vial speaks of the precious-

ness of the prayers of the saints which were offered upon the golden altar, which is before the throne of God.
Again it is interesting to note that prayer performs supernatural activities both in heaven and on earth. Prayers are described as incense that goes before the Throne of God. On being received they are mingled with fire, and are sent back to the earth where they begin to cause voices, thundering, lightning, and earthquake.

Prayers that are offered by the saints come back to fulfil the request they were originally sent out for. The original requests, upon reaching the throne of God are empowered with supernatural grace to speak back to situations that they were intended to transform. Only this time they will be carrying a supernatural ability of dynamic power, earthquake, and lighting. There are many incidents in the Bible that had these results when the saints of the Lord prayed.

And when they had prayed, the place was shaken where they were assembled together; and they were all filled with the Holy Ghost, and they spake the word of God with boldness. (Acts 4:31)

This is another example of the result of prayer that can shake a place supernaturally. In the Old Testament, Samuel prayed to the Lord when they were faced with opposition and literally a sound of thunder was heard. This ties in with the picture we saw in the book of Revelation where the prayers of the saints were being mingled with earthquake, thunder, fire, and lightning.

As Samuel was offering up the burnt offering, the Philistines approached for the battle against Israel. Then the Lord thundered with a great voice that day against the Philistines and threw them into confusion, and they were defeated and fled before Israel. (1 Samuel 7:10)

Samuel's prayers for Israel were accompanied by God's voice of thunder, another clear illustration of how prayer brings God's voice from heaven to interfere in the affairs of his servants as His response to prayer.
In the case of Samuel, the Philistines were confused upon hearing a voice of thunder that came from heaven. Our God thunders from heaven.

As Samuel was offering up the burnt offering, the Philistines approached for the battle against Israel. Then the Lord thunred with a great voice that day against the Philistines and threw them into confusion, and they were defeated and fled before Israel. (1 Samuel 7:10)

The above scripture speaks of the God of Glory who thunders. When our God speaks to situations from his glory, thunder is released. Hence the prayers of His children when they reach His throne get empowered with the 'thunder element' to come back and confront the situations on earth with amplified supernatural power.

For thus saith the Lord of hosts; Yet once, it is a little while, and I will shake the heavens, and the earth, and the sea, and the dry land; (Haggai 2:1)

God promised through the mouth of His prophet Haggai that one more time He was going to shake the heavens and the earth. God shakes the heavens and earth through the prayers of the saints that He supernaturally uses to bring His shaking. 'Heavens' refers to the realm of demonic operations. As we fight with principalities in heavenly places they will be shaken because of the prayers of the saints.

Whose voice then shook the earth: but now he hath promised, saying, Yet once more I shake not the earth only, but also heaven. (Hebrews 12:26)

The Lord Jesus' prayer on the cross had a similar effect that caused the elements to shake and quake. The power of prayer from the Son of God Himself during a difficult time caused heavens to respond this way:

And [at once] the veil [of the Holy of Holies] of the temple was [a]torn in two from top to bottom; the earth shook and the rocks were split apart. (Matthew 27:51)

In short; prayers are amplified beyond their frame upon arriving before the throne of God. Judging from what we gather in the above scriptures these prayers get mingled with a supernatural element of fire, thunder, and earthquake. So indeed prayers are supernatural and they play a pivotal role in the affairs of mankind on earth, but first of all, they must be offered before God in order for them to receive the supernatural input. It is for man to pray, and God to answer, as promised in His word. When man call God's promise is that He will answer them.

Hitherto have ye asked nothing in my name: ask, and ye shall receive, that your joy may be full. (John 16:24)

I am a strong believer in the fact that prayers are recorded in heaven, at some point they build up and release God's mandate on the earth, just as is in heaven. God does that in response to the prayers of the saints. It is, therefore, important to know that in the fullness of time God will respond. It may be sooner or later, but the prayers will be answered in a supernatural fashion and as I said, from that moment on history is changed forever. It takes prayer for the supernatural power of God to be released. Even angels are released from heaven in response to prayer, just as in the case of Peter.

PETER'S SUPERNATURAL ESCAPE THROUGH THE AID OF AN ANGEL

Peter, was kept in prison: therefore prayer was made without ceasing by the church unto God for him. And when Herod would have brought him forth, the same night Peter was sleeping between two soldiers, bound with two chains: and the keepers before the door kept the prison.

And, behold, the angel of the Lord came upon him, and a light shined in the prison: and he smote Peter on the side, and raised him up, saying, Arise up quickly. And his chains fell off from his hands. (Acts 12:5-7)

This incident provides us with some insight into what happens in the spiritual realm that causes the eternal God to intervene in the affairs of mankind. Peter was incarcerated for the preaching of the gospel and was set to appear before a court of law and face the king. While he was being kept under the watchful eyes of the soldiers, corporate prayers were made for him by the Church unto God. The prayers were so insistent that reference to those prayers was that they were made without ceasing. The result of these prayers was that an angel came to Peter and released him from prison by way of supernatural manifestation. Corporate prayers release supernatural activities, this is not just a Bible story this is what actually took place.

When the saints of the Lord begin to pray angels are dispatched to interfere and distract the enemy and set the people of God free. The interesting part of the story is that angels get involved, and it is important to know whenever angels show up they carry the presence of God, therefore, what they accomplish is supernatural. So his escape from prison through the aid of an angel was a result of prayer, not just any prayer, but supernatural prayer. Peter was a blessed man indeed as we see him here as a beneficiary of corporate prayer. The whole church understood that the role of his ministry was one of the foundation stones of the New Testament movement.
He depended on their prayers so that his spiritual assignment was not compromised, I am reminded of Jesus telling Peter how the enemy had planned to destroy Peter but gave him assurance that He would pray for him.

And the Lord said, Simon, Simon, behold, Satan hath desired to have you, that he may sift you as wheat: (Luke 22:31)

Jesus prayed for Peter and instructed him that when he finally escaped Satan he must go and encourage others. So when the church was praying for Peter they were in agreement with Jesus. Peter was a custodian of the prophetic word of encouragement to the world that was going through discouragement from Satan and his evil forces. This can only be defused by those that have a mandate from heaven to speak to their God.

But [on the other hand] the one who prophesies speaks to people for edification [to promote their spiritual growth] and [speaks words of] encouragement [to uphold and advise them concerning the matters of God] and [speaks words of] consolation [to compassionately comfort them].
(1 Corinthians 14:3)

But it is mandatory that the church prays for such that are carriers of the sure word of prophecy and encouragement in order for their testimony not to be derailed.

DANIEL FASTED FOR TWENTY-ONE DAYS AND AN ANGEL CAME DOWN

I ate no pleasant bread, neither came flesh nor wine in my mouth, neither did I anoint myself at all, till three whole weeks were fulfilled.
(Daniel 10:3)

Above is the outcome of a twenty-one-day consecration which Daniel undertook. It was a three-week prayer and fasting that resulted in an angel being dispatched from the Throne of God.

And he said unto me, O Daniel, a man greatly beloved, understand the words that I speak unto thee, and stand upright: for unto thee am I now sent. And when he had spoken this word unto me, I stood to tremble. Then said he unto me, Fear not, Daniel: for from the first day that thou didst set thine heart to understand, and to chasten thyself before thy God, thy words were heard, and I am come for thy words. (Daniel 10:11-12)

This is another exciting supernatural activity that prayer can accomplish. The angels began to download the day he started praying. God heard his prayers and the angel was sent in response to his prayers for wisdom and understanding. Prayer unlocks heaven's secrets and causes men to tap into the supernatural realm. Daniel was one of the privileged few who were given the opportunity to be visited by one of the heavenly hosts. A highly ranked angel showed up and another was sent to help him. Daniel's natural body could not stand the Angel's presence and he was overwhelmed by this supernatural experience. The whole chapter is full of the trauma of Daniel who could not stand the presence of this high ranked Angel that had come in response to his prayer. True prayer brings Heaven's presence into the now. From experience, we found that when heavenly beings appear in a prayer service, or, in a church gathering the whole place is charged by what is indescribable 'electric' presence of the supernatural. This is the Presence of God that the natural body cannot handle; it feels overwhelmed and in most cases responds by falling down, or, breaking down in tears of Holy reverence.

Prayer ushers people into the realm of the supernatural and causes them to understand the hidden things. It reveals the course of the world affairs and the direction of events that would transpire in the near future. This was seen in Daniel. We see supporting scriptures revealing the same pattern with similar occurrences. Angels are supernatural beings that are always associated with, or, connected to prayers that the saints offer be-fore God. And Cornelius said, Four days ago I was fasting until this hour, and at the ninth hour I prayed in my house, and, behold, a man stood before me in bright clothing,

And said, Cornelius, thy prayer is heard, and thine alms are had in remembrance in the sight of God. (Acts 10:30-31)

Cornelius had a similar encounter to Daniel, where a man stood in white before him after some days of fasting and prayer. He then revealed to him what God intended to do in the coming days.
Prayers will never go unnoticed. They are filed and recorded and they are supernatural. They are like fire starters that cause heaven's dynamite to explode thus causing the elements and the forces of darkness and strongholds to disappear permanently.

THE HOLY SPIRIT IS A PRAYER AID FOR SUPERNATURAL PRAYER

Likewise the Spirit also helpeth our infirmities: for we know not what we should pray for as we ought: but the Spirit itself maketh intercession for us with groanings which cannot be uttered. (Romans 8:26)

As quoted from the book of Romans this scripture speaks of our infirmities. It seeks to describe how insignificant we are when it comes to articulating prayer. Only the spirit of God provides us with the proper spiritual vocabulary which is in line with God's will and purpose. Holy Spirit led prayers are those that the Spirit of God helps us with when we approach the throne of God in prayer. This means that it is only through the Spirit of God that we can be empowered with spiritual aid that will strengthen us to pray as we should. We are limited by our infirmities.

Here is how the Webster dictionary defines the word: "infirmity";
"the state of being infirm; feebleness; an imperfection or weakness; especially an unsound, unhealthy, or debilitated state."
I am convinced that the scripture is trying to explain that the Spirit knows the state of our weaknesses; according to the Bible we cannot articulate prayer as natural beings, therefore He works as our mediator to express what we need in a manner or fashion that is guaranteed to cause God to respond. The scripture also addresses the fact that we do not know what we should pray for as we ought, in other words, our natural abilities do not possess accurate understanding on what to activate before the throne of God. It takes the Spirit of God who knows God, and who understands God, to pray through us and pour through us groaning's which we cannot utter, In verse 27 the Scripture says:

The spirit searches the heart and what is in the mind of the spirit and he prays for the saints according to the will of God. (Romans 8:27)

It takes the spirit of God to pray spiritual prayers in accordance with the

will and purpose of God that establishes supernaturalism.
Hence the book of Romans clearly states that when we pray our wording is not sufficiently accurate and our articulations fall short of expressing ourselves properly. We thank God that in His wisdom He has given us an aid, the Holy Spirit, to help us when we pray. I always say to people in my little experience of praying effective prayers, I've come to the conclusion that it is not in the quantity of my words, or, the accuracy of my words that causes heaven to move on my behalf. Most of the time my long prayers obtain no results. It is the simple and earnest prayers that are directed by the Holy Spirit that produce dynamic results. The prayers that are prayed by us when the Holy Spirit, has given us a prayer with supernatural wording are very effective.

We are told that Jesus, after being baptized, was led by the Spirit to be tested of the devil. This is one of the classic encounters between Satan and Jesus. As the story unfolds Jesus prevailed victoriously, and the key is that He was led by the Holy Spirit into that encounter. Holy Ghost led prayers bring guaranteed answers and Holy Ghost led battles never fail. The book of Romans says we do not know how to pray and it is true; we do not, our natural way of praying is not effective at all. The Holy Ghost must pray through us with the proper wording, only then can we experience the supernatural power that is activated by the Holy Spirit.

SOLOMON'S SUPERNATURAL PRAYER FOR WISDOM

This prayer is often referred to the prayer of Solomon, many renowned teachers and preachers use this to refer to how Solomon asked God for wisdom and God granted it to him. But another look into the story will reveal some interesting things. Solomon was sleeping at the time. If he was sleeping how would he have prayed in his sleep? Can one pray in his sleep? Don't we have to be conscious in our praying? If the answer is yes then how can we say Solomon prayed. I am not discounting that prayer was offered and in turn, God granted him what he requested. However, I'd like to add this that it was not a natural prayer that Solomon prayed. It was a supernatural prayer that tapped into the spiritual realm and connected him with God.

God inspired the prayer and then supernaturally answered it and gave Solomon not only wisdom but riches and honour. As seen in this story God's elevation was through prayer, but not a prayer that was produced out of his intellect, but from the Spirit of God.

REFLECTION AND PRAYER ACTIVATION

1. What must you do if you want to be healed through prayer? Therefore, ______________ your sins to one another [your false steps, your offences], and pray for one another, that you may be________and________. The heartfelt and persistent prayer of a righteous man (believer) can accomplish much [when put into action and made effective by God—it is dynamic and can have tremendous power].

2. If you call on the Lord what will He do in response? Call to Me and ______________ you, and tell you [and even show you] __________and __________things, [things which have been confined and hidden], which you do not know and understand and cannot distinguish.

3. According to the Book of Revelation where do your prayers go? And when he had taken the book, the four beasts and four and twenty elders fell down before the Lamb, having every one of them harps, and ________full of________, which are the_________of saints."

4. What happened in response to the prayers offered in Acts 4 v 31? And when they had prayed, the place was_________where they were assembled together; and they were all ________, and they_________the word of God with boldness.

5. What happened when Daniel prayed in Daniel chapter 10? And he said unto me, O Daniel, a man greatly beloved, understand the words that I speak unto thee, and stand upright: for unto thee am I now sent. And when he had spoken this word unto me, I stood to tremble. Then said he

unto me,____________ , Daniel: for from the first day that thou didst set thine heart to___________, and to chasten thyself before thy God, thy words were heard, and I am come for thy words.

6.What does the Holy Spirit do when you pray? And how? The spirit the heart and what is in the mind of the spirit and he________for the saints according to the ___________ of God

7. Why does Holy spirit help you when you pray? Likewise the Spirit also ____________ our infirmities: for we know not what we should pray for as we ought: but the Spirit itself maketh ________for us with ________ which cannot be uttered.

PRAYER

Lord, I call on You that if there are any secret sins in my heart that I've done aware or unaware I confess them before you. Reveal to me things that I don't know that may be hidden in my heart I bring my prayer before your throne, may you send thunder and earthquake to destabilize my enemy shake everything that has become a strong hold in my life and grant me boldness, spirit of revelation and angelic accompaniment anoint me with your Holy Spirit and power to pray according to your will I ask all this in the name of Jesus amen.

CHAPTER 8

SUPERNATURAL DELIVERANCE

When we look at the word deliverance from the Hebrew dictionary it is the word 'Pallet' which speaks of escape or deliverance. It is interesting to note that every born-again child of God has escaped the wrath of eternal damnation by accepting Jesus as the Lord and Savior as the Bible declares that those that believe in Him will not die, but have everlasting life.

Jesus said unto her, I am the resurrection, and the life: he that believeth in me, though he were dead, yet shall he live: And whosoever liveth and believeth in me shall never die. Believest thou this? (John 11:25-26)

Every believer will not be condemned, every non-believer will not escape eternal judgment. Jesus brought deliverance and He provided a way of escape.

The Greek word for deliverance is 'aphesis' which speaks of freedom, pardon, forgiveness, liberty, and remission.
Jesus is the only one who can provide true freedom, it is sad to know that

many people who profess to have known the truth have found nothing but religion. Religion cannot offer freedom and because of this people are not delivered. One can continue to be a religious person without having experienced true freedom. Jesus is the only one who can provide remission of sins and true liberty. Forgiveness is embodied in his Name, as the Bible declares that if the Son shall set you free you shall be free indeed.

If the Son therefore shall make you free, ye shall be free indeed. (John 8:36)

Zechariah, the father of John, prophesied about Jesus that God was going to grant deliverance through Him and freedom from our enemies that we would serve him without fear.

That he would grant unto us, that we being delivered out of the hand of our enemies might serve him without fear (Luke 1:74)

One of the attributes that deliverance provides is freedom from fear and it ushers one into a realm of joy that is indescribable. Part of Zechariah's prophecy alluded to the fact that Jesus was going to sit on the throne of his father David. David in the Old Testament represented the deliverance of God; if one can recall, David was anointed to fight battles that brought freedom to the people of God. One of his remarkable battles was his fight with the giant Goliath. The entire nation was afraid when they ran out of options, but David was the one that God raised and he led the people of

God out of that difficult era. This is what David had to say in one of his songs:

Thou art my hiding place; thou shalt preserve me from trouble; thou shalt compass me about with songs of deliverance. Selah. (Psalms 32:7)

David alluded to the fact that God was his hiding place. He went on to say He provided protection from trouble. It is true that freedom and protection from life's challenges, is only found in God. He also continued to say, "You surround me with songs and shouts of deliverance." One of the signs of a delivered person is joy, most of the time when people are happy they sing. David connects the singing that was brought about by deliverance, not only singing, but shouts. It is interesting to note that the day when he fought and defeated the giant Goliath the ladies composed a song in which they expressed their gratitude for the deliverance of that day.

And the women answered one another as they played, and said, Saul, hath slain his thousands, and David his ten thousand.
(1 Samuel 18:7)

Deliverance indeed brings songs of celebration to the one delivered. It is impossible to keep quiet when God has come through for you and you have escaped from a difficult situation. As you know that it was beyond your human ability to come out of it, when you acknowledge that it took the supernatural hand of God, you will shout and sing, "the Webster dictionary describes 'deliverance' as an act of bringing forth children."

In the maternity ward, there are shouts and cries that takes place, those are shouts because there is deliverance that takes place. The deliverance that says new life is coming to the earth, and some shouts of pushing and cries from the child announcing 'I am here'. When God forgives our sins, when God brings us to a place of liberty, supernaturally it is impossible to keep quiet. Paul, the Apostle, mentioned something very profound in relation to deliverance. He asked, "Who shall deliver me?" Seemingly deliverance requires that someone administers it to you. Sometimes it might require a fellow believer, or someone who has a relationship with God, to administer supernatural deliverance over one's life. Hence, Paul used the words "who shall deliver me?"; his statement is a question. Is it possible that people are not delivered because they do not seek for it? How can you be delivered unless you acknowledge that there are areas in your life that require deliverance therefore there is a need to identify areas in one's life that need supernatural deliverance to be administered to. Hence Paul alluded to these words.

O wretched man that I am! who shall deliver me from the body of this death? (Romans 7:24)

The scripture above is a build up of the expression of how Paul felt and how he could not keep the law of Moses. He said every time he wanted to do right he failed and every time he wanted to do good, evil was present.

He went on to to identify the position he found himself in and described it as "wretched."

A study of the word 'wretched' from the Webster dictionary it means: very miserable, sunk in, or accompanied by distress, as from want, anxiety, or grief; calamitous, woeful, very afflicting.
He said he wanted someone to deliver him because he was very miserable. We live in a time where there is a lot of misconception about deliverance. There are so many people who claim to be deliverance workers and they claim methods, ideas and prescriptions that have no proven record. A follow up on some of the things they claim proves to be otherwise. I've seen and heard of some weird methods and when you ask them why they do what they do in the name of deliverance you would find out that they do not have a clue. They use man made methods and religious methods that cannot deliver a soul. However, Paul prescribes deliverance when he goes on to explain in the following verse:

I thank God through Jesus Christ our Lord. So then with the mind, I myself serve the law of God; but with the flesh the law of sin. (Romans7:25)

The verse 25 is the solution that Paul prescribes. It is that Jesus Christ our Lord is a deliverer; supernatural deliverance only comes through Jesus Christ. When Jesus came to Nazareth to his home town where he was born, he went to the synagogue where he stood up, opened the book of Isaiah and said the following:

The Spirit of the Lord is upon me, because he hath anointed me to preach the gospel to the poor; he hath sent me to heal the brokenhearted, to preach deliverance to the captives, and recovering of sight to the blind, to set at liberty them that are bruised, (Luke 4:18)

Genuine supernatural deliverance is only found in the name of Jesus. Jesus came to set the captive free, and the gospel that we preach carries deliverance grace. Man is a tripartite being with a spirit, soul and body. Before we got saved we opened our souls and our bodies to be oppressed by demons. The day we came to surrender our lives to Jesus, our spirit man was saved. Believers cannot be possessed by demons, but they can be oppressed by demons, even after they get saved. There is need to identify areas in their lives that the enemy may have found entry bringing bondage. These areas need deliverance, there is need for continuous deliverance in the lives of every born-again child of God.

Stand fast therefore in the liberty wherewith Christ hath made us free, and be not entangled again with the yoke of bondage. (Galatians 5:1)

It is possible that if there is neglect that one might open demonic bondage again and the enemy can come in and take control, therefore there is a need for one to continuously go through true biblical deliverance.
The Bible speaks a great deal about deliverance, despite the misconceptions of the doctrines of man and the doctrines of devils. In the scripture below:

And these signs shall follow them that believe; In my name shall they cast out devils; they shall speak with new tongues; (Mark 16:17)

Jesus said these signs shall follow them that believe, therefore deliverance is a supernatural sign that follows every believer. He says they will cast out devils in the name of Jesus. This means to 'eject' and to remove every demonic influence in a life that was possessed by evil spirits. For instance, there is a case of a man that was possessed by evil spirits and when Jesus came to the man He began to administer deliverance to him. Before He administered deliverance to him He first identified the demons that were operating in his life.

And he asked him, What is thy name? And he answered, saying, My name is Legion: for we are many. (Mark 5:9)

There is need to identify areas in one's life that have suffered possession and the oppression of the enemy. It is a supernatural administration that requires a supernatural operation and this can only be done where the correct spiritual diagnosis has taken place. In the case of the man who had a Legion of demons, when Jesus had finally cast them out he was seen sitting at the feet of Jesus, he was ready to follow Jesus and to become part of His is team. Would it be possible that people that find themselves not willing to follow the way of salvation do so because there is a demonic hindrance that prevents them from fully surrendering and sitting at the feet of Jesus to serve Him. Casting out of devils is a supernatural activity and it's a sign that the kingdom of God has been demonstrated. It speaks of the proof of the God who is the Highest, who has power over evil and any other power that may try to raise up against His creation. Jesus alluded to this:

But if I with the finger of God cast out devils, no doubt the kingdom of God is come upon you. (Luke 11:20)

The kingdom of God is the only kingdom that has the supernatural power of casting out devils. Demons are subject to Jesus; the Bible says Jesus was anointed with the Holy Spirit and power and He went about healing the sick and setting free those that were oppressed by demons.

How God anointed Jesus of Nazareth with the Holy Ghost and with power: who went about doing good and healing all that were oppressed of the devil; for God was with him. (Acts 10:38)

Demons, what are they? They are evil spirits without bodies, they are part of the fallen angels that were cast out together with Lucifer when he rebelled against God in heaven. They do not have bodies to function here on earth as only humans were designed with bodies that are fit to live here on earth. The fallen angels usurp their way into human's life by possessing and oppressing them so that they can continue their rebellious and evil agendas while they are awaiting the final judgment which is hell. They are

continuously in search of human bodies to possess.
It is only in the kingdom of God that God has raised deliverance workers full of the Holy Ghost who can cast them out, and bring freedom to the children of God. There is an incident in The Old testament that involves David worshipping by playing the harp. It served as a deliverance ministry because it is said that the evil spirit that possessed king Saul departed whenever he played the harp.

And it came to pass, when the evil spirit from God was upon Saul, that David took an harp, and played with his hand: so Saul was refreshed, and was well, and the evil spirit departed from him. (1 Samuel 16:23)

Demons cannot stand when worship takes place and they have no choice but to leave. An environment of worship and prayer is very toxic to the kingdom of darkness and it makes demons uncomfortable as they cannot stand it. Supernatural deliverance is for today. It is known as God's children's bread. Every child of God can partake of it; it is the right of every child of God who is born into the kingdom of God to be set free from demonic interference.

REFLECTION AND PRAYER ACTIVATION

1. What did Jesus say He was? Jesus said unto her, I am the________, and the________: he that believeth in me, though he were dead, yet shall he live: And whosoever _________and _________ in me shall never die. Believest thou this?

2. What was Zechariah's prophecy concerning Jesus? That he would __________unto us, that we being _________out of the hand of our enemies might serve him without ________________.

3. This is what David had to say in one of his songs. Thou art_________ my________ ; thou shalt preserve me from_________; thou shalt compass me about with songs of __________. Selah.

4. Paul said who shall deliver me? O___________man that I am! who shall deliver me from the__________death?

5. What did Jesus say when he came to Nazareth when he stood in the synagogues. The Spirit of the_________is upon me, because he hath _________ me to preach the gospel to the poor; he hath sent me to heal the brokenhearted, to preach____________ , and recovering of sight to the blind, to set at__________ them that are bruised

6. What signs shall follow them that believe? And these ________shall follow them that believe; In my name shall they__________-devils; they shall speak with____________

7.What did David's music do for King Saul? And it came to pass,_______ when the evil spirit from God was upon Saul, that David took an________, , and played with his hand: so Saul was__________, and was well, and the __________from him.

1. John 11:25 -26 [KJV]
2. Luke 1:74 [KJV]
3. Psalms 32:7 [KJV]
4. Romans 7:24 [KJV]
5. Luke 4:18 [KJV]
6. Mark 16:17 [KJV]
7. 1 Samuel 16:23 [KJV]

PRAYER

Jesus I want to thank you for resurrection, I was dead in my transgressions without God without hope. I thank you that you have delivered me from the powers of darkness and you have translated me to the kingdom of light. You have saved me from the kingdom of darkness and from fear and you have made me a child of God. Preserve my soul and continuously fill me with songs of deliverance, fill me with praises and your joy. I thank you that you have set me free from captivity and you've filled me with your Holy Spirit and power. I thank you that you have given me power to cast out devils that in your name even poison will not harm me I will trample over the powers of hell thank you God that your deliverance has found me, Amen.

CHAPTER 9

SUPERNATURAL GIVING

The bible is decorated with many exciting references regarding giving. In most cases where giving is mentioned or where giving took place God's supernatural power was evidently demonstrated. One would say giving is a direct trigger of supernatural happenings. Giving among believers is divinely connected to the God of the supernatural. Giving is a blessed exercise as the bible alludes that God loves a cheerful giver.

But this I say, He which soweth sparingly shall reap also sparingly; and he which soweth bountifully shall reap also bountifully. Every man according as he purposeth in his heart, so let him give; not grudgingly, or of necessity: for God loveth a cheerful giver.
(2 Corinthians 9:6-7)

Giving should not be a burden but a blessing and it must always be accompanied with joyfulness only then will the one that gives experience the miracles that accompanies it. The amount of one's sowing will determine how much he is going to harvest. The miracle of seed sowing derives from the heart of cheerfulness versus the heart that gives out of the cold sense of duty which the scripture above has said giving grudgingly and out of necessity. One should never give because he had been told to do so. One should give with a heart that understands that the principle that underlines giving is connected to God. God looks into the heart as we have seen in the scripture and loves the heart of those that give cheerfully. The opposite is also very true that those that do not give cheerfully are working in direct disagreement with what God looks for. Renowned men and women of the Bible were great givers. It proves that they had a relationship with the God who is a giver. One can never love God and not give. To have a relationship with God will put you in a place where you always want to pour more to those that need as part of your expression and appreciation for God's creation. We are an extension of the hand of God and His heart, His love, and His tender care for creation. There are many people who are hurting, who are in need, whom, God wants us to touch on His behalf, to love on His behalf and to care on His behalf. It is the duty of every child of God to play an ambassadorial role of representing God through giving. It is important to note that our giving reveals that we are representing our Giving Father. The Bible has this to say:

For God is the one who provides seed for the farmer and then bread to eat. In the same way, he will provide and increase your resources and then produce a great harvest of generosity[a] in you. (2 Corinthians 9:10 NLT)

Giving is seeding and harvesting is the result of sowing, therefore, if there is a time of sowing there will be harvest time. Harvest is the result of your sowing system and those that do not experience the harvest in their life lacked the opportunity to put seed in their ground. After you have harvested you need to put aside quality seed for the season ahead. A wise farmer does not rest on the past harvest; he looks into the future by sowing seed in order to have a future harvest.

While the earth remaineth, seedtime and harvest, and cold and heat, and summer and winter, and day and night shall not cease. (Genesis 8:22)

Giving is a principle that God established to bless His people, man will only reap based on what they have sown, and therefore it is a reaping and sowing principle. If you don't sow you won't reap and if you don't give you will not get, as the Bible declares if you give, it shall be given unto you.

Give, and it shall be given unto you; good measure, pressed down, and shaken together, and running over, shall men give into your bosom. For with the same measure that ye mete withal it shall be measured to you again. (Luke 6:38)

ABRAHAM AND REVELATORY GIVING

If you want good measures that are pressed down and shaken together and running over to be given to you then you need to sow seed accordingly, God will direct people who are designated to provide your harvest, if you have been found faithful in your sowing, God will always move men to give back into your life, but it all starts with the activation your seed produces. Abraham was a great giver, it is recorded that he paid his tithe to Melchisedec when he was on his way back home after rescuing his nephew Lot. His tithe also covered Levi who was still yet unborn in his loins. Typically, Abraham's descendants partook of the blessing of Abraham's giving while they were not yet born.

And as I may so say, Levi also, who receiveth tithes, paid tithes in Abraham. For he was yet in the loins of his father when Melchisedec met him. (Hebrews 7:8-9)

He gave by revelation, and giving requires revelation. Revelation is spiritual insight and most who struggle with giving lack the understanding of what giving can bring about. Giving can bless future generations as seen in the above scripture that Abraham descendants enjoyed perpetual blessing from the giving of their father. He was not taught how to give by any Bible preacher because there was no Bible during the time of Abraham. If there was a Bible he could have compared scriptures and the notes of other people who gave, however, in this case, it was a divine inspiration that taught him how to give, it was a supernatural insight he received from God. That connected him to something so profound that the Bible says God called him his friend,

And the scripture was fulfilled which saith, Abraham believed God, and it

was imputed unto him for righteousness: and he was called the Friend of God. (James 2:23)

There was a reason why God called him his friend, God is a giving God. When you begin to walk in giving you are revealing one of God's attributes. Two can walk together as friends only when they agree together. You cannot be tight-fisted and expect to flow with the generous Spirit of God. Friends agree in their spirit and hearts. They are of one spirit.

And the LORD said, Shall I hide from Abraham that thing which I do; (Genesis 18:17)

Givers are custodians of God's divine secrets. Heaven is a giving heaven, God has one son, and He made him a seed to harvest the whole world.

For God so loved the world, that he gave his only begotten Son, that whosoever believeth in him should not perish, but have everlasting life. (John 3:16)

Jesus taught that the birds of the air have no fields to plant, and yet our heavenly father takes care of them.

Behold the fowls of the air: for they sow not, neither do they reap nor gather into barns; yet your heavenly Father feedeth them. Are ye not much better than they? (Matthew 6:26)

One cannot claim that he is born again if he does not understand the principle of giving. The church began with the one that was given, who died and rose again. God is a loving and giving God and loves those that love and give. You cannot love without giving, though you can give with- out loving. True giving derives from pure love. The essence of pure giving is supernatural. The New Testament church grew on a daily basis because it was a giving church. It became a growing church; a community that loves and gives grows. It was a multiracial generous community, full of love for one another and accompanied by supernatural miracles, and signs and wonders, and attracted all kinds of people from all walks of life.

True givers don't discriminate as there is no more Greek nor Jew, the New Testament community had widows of different ethnic groups that were catered for without regard to where they came from.

And in those days, when the number of the disciples was multiplied, there arose a murmuring of the Grecians against the Hebrews, because their widows were neglected in the daily ministration. (Acts 6:1)

The scripture below speaks of an army general whose name was Cornelius, and this what the Bible had to say about him

And said, Cornelius, thy prayer is heard, and thine alms are had in remembrance in the sight of God. (Acts 10:31)

He was a giver and a prayer warrior, giving and praying are twins. True giving must be God-directed, one must know what he is giving or else it won't be accepted by God. Hence prayer plays a pivotal role in assuring that one does not give amiss. Cornelius gave, and his giving penetrated the heavens and caused God's attention to come upon him. This is what God had to say about him, "his prayers, his alms were remembered." We should never overlook the power of our giving; like our prayers, our giving is always recorded. We should always pray for God-directed giving, and such giving produces supernatural activity. The story of Cornelius and the supernatural activity which opened heaven's blessing are clearly related. His giving moved God to respond with a massive harvest. Cornelius became the first Gentile to experience the baptism of the Holy Spirit in history. It all begun with giving and while he was in prayer he had an angelic visitation announcing to him that his giving has caused God to send to him one of the apostles who was going to reveal more to him about the supernatural. When Peter arrived, and saw God's outpouring he had to confess that God is not a respecter of persons, which means that God responded to his giving, not his status. Cornelius' experience was activated by supernatural activity triggered by his giving.

Then Peter opened his mouth, and said, Of a truth, I perceive that God is no respecter of persons: But in every nation, he that feareth him, and worketh righteousness, is accepted with him. (Acts 10:34-35)

His giving was announced from heaven, what happens in the natural can trigger the supernatural invasion of our circumstances. Giving reveals what is in our hearts; if your heart is full of God's love, giving becomes the norm. As I said earlier on you cannot love without giving, and giving is always motivated from a heart that is overflowing with the love of God. The Bible declares that God loves a cheerful giver, giving and cheerfulness work hand in hand.

But this I say, He which soweth sparingly shall reap also sparingly; and he which soweth bountifully shall reap also bountifully. Every man according as he purposeth in his heart, so let him give; not grudgingly, or of necessity: for God loveth a cheerful. (2 Corinthians 9:6-7)

THE QUALITY GIVER VS THE QUANTITY

There is a woman in the New Testament during the time of Jesus' ministry, who gave an outstanding offering that caught the attention of Jesus. What is amazing in this story it's not the amount she gave, it was the quality of the giving. I would like to call her a supernatural giver because this is the giving that got Jesus talking. He was deeply impressed and moved by her action. The reason being she gave from her heart. Jesus calls to His disciples to Him, He said to them;

I assure you and most solemnly say to you, this poor widow put in [proportionally] more than all the contributors to the treasury. For they all contributed from their surplus, but she, from her poverty, put in all she had, all she had to live on. (Mark 12:43-44, AMP)

The kind of giving that touches heaven and causes miracles to happen is the giving that is sacrificial and that is given from the heart. It is given in faith, to honour and glorify God, it is the kind of giving that says God is my Source. I give as a seed with the understanding that I will harvest in due time, I may be sowing in tears, but I will reap in joy.

A MEAL OFFERING

There are so many types of giving in the Bible. We have heard of the giving that Cornelius gave, that was remembered by heaven. We just spoke on the passage above the woman who gave and Jesus made some remarks about it. Below is a classic story of a woman who gave a meal, in turn, the meal produced a supernatural harvest. This incident took place during the time of famine when a prophet visited the widow and her son. These were hard times, not only for the widow and her son but the entire nation. When the prophet of God came he released a word to this widow, the word was concerning an offering of a meal. One might call it a meal offering and the woman in response alluded to the fact that she only had one last meal.

And as she was going to fetch it, he called to her, and said, Bring me, I pray thee, a morsel of bread in thine hand. And she said, As the LORD thy God liveth, I have not a cake, but an handful of meal in a barrel, and a little oil in a cruse: and, behold, I am gathering two sticks, that I may go in and dress it for me and my son, that we may eat it, and die. (1 Kings 17:11-12)

But the prophet of God continued to insist that the meal offering be made and that he would eat it first, and afterward, he would bless them. As the story unfolds the meal led the prophet to pray for a miracle that brought a surplus into this household. It sustained her and her child throughout the duration of the famine.

For thus saith the LORD God of Israel, The barrel of meal shall not waste, neither shall the cruse of oil fail, until the day that the LORD sendeth rain upon the earth. And she went and did according to the saying of Elijah: and she, and he, and her house, did eat many days. (1 Kings 17: 14 – 15)

Giving produces the supernatural provision of God, giving is supernatural. It releases life, just like a sown seed. Throughout the Bible miracles of God's multiplication of meals were performed supernaturally. There are incidences of miracles that were triggered by just a meal. Giving is designed to produce a harvest. This principle of sowing and reaping is a supernatural principle. One might say, but this was in the Old Testament. God's dealings with His children are not limited by time. God is the same God, what He did in the Old Testament, He also did in the New Testament, and He continues to be the same God who performs supernatural acts whenever the same principles are applied.

Jesus provided supernatural meals in His ministry. One took place when the people that Jesus was ministering to became hungry. He wanted to feed them and He then requested for anyone who had food. A young man offered his meal, and Jesus took that offering. He used it to feed a multitude and gave the giver back several baskets full of bread and fish to take home. Jesus literally multiplied it and then having used it gave him much more than he had originally given to Jesus. It came back multiplied. It is known as a miracle of five loaves and two fishes.

And they say unto him, We have here but five loaves, and two fishes. He said, Bring them hither to me. And he commanded the multitude to sit down on the grass, and took the five loaves, and the two fishes, and looking up to heaven, he blessed, and brake, and gave the loaves to his disciples and the disciples to the multitude. And they did all eat, and were filled: and they took up of the fragments that remained twelve baskets full. (Matthew 14:17-20)

After they had eaten there was a surplus left, which again demonstrates that God can supply more than our expectations. In most cases where food miracles occurred, there was a multiplication of what was initially given so whatever we give God multiplies it. Giving is just a seed that triggers abundance, if you want more than what you have, then you must release it as a seed.

Similarly, another woman in the Old Testament at a place called Shumen purposed in her heart to build a room for a prophet of God.

Let us make a little chamber, I pray thee, on the wall; and let us set for

him there a bed, and a table, and a stool, and a candlestick: and it shall be, when he cometh to us, that he shall turn in thither. And it fell on a day, that he came thither, and he turned into the chamber and lay there.
(2 Kings 4:10-11)

As a result, the prophet of God prayed for her situation as she was barren. God gave them a miracle child. This was His response to what she triggered by the construction of a guest room for the man of God.

And he said unto him, Say now unto her, Behold, thou hast been careful for us with all this care; what is to be done for thee? wouldest thou be spoken for to the king, or to the captain of the host? And she answered I dwell among mine own people. And he said, What then is to be done for her? And Gehazi answered, Verily she hath no child, and her husband is old. And he said, Call her. And when he had called her, she stood in the door. And he said, About this season, according to the time of life, thou shalt embrace a son. And she said, Nay, my lord, thou man of God, do not lie unto thine handmaid. And the woman conceived, and bare a son at that season that Elisha had said unto her, according to the time of life.
(2 Kings 4:13-17)

It is interesting to note that giving can activate things that were not functional to become functional. Barrenness was broken, a miracle baby was born. At some point when the child grew up, he got sick one day and died the same day.

And when the child was grown, it fell on a day, that he went out to his father to the reapers. And he said unto his father, My head, my head. And he said to a lad, Carry him to his mother. And when he had taken him and brought him to his mother, he sat on her knees till noon and then died. (2 Kings 4:18-20)

This woman by faith refused to accept her child's death, and travelled to the prophet. She insisted that the prophet came with her, and he prayed for the child and the child came back to life.

Then he returned, and walked in the house to and fro; and went up, and stretched himself upon him: and the child sneezed seven times, and the child opened his eyes. And he called Gehazi, and said, Call this Shunammite. So he called her. And when she came in unto him, he said, Take up thy son. Then she went in, and fell at his feet, and bowed herself to the ground, and took up her son, and went out.

(2 Kings 4:35-37)

This became a double miracle and she lived to testify that God gave her a child and when the child died, God brought back the child from the dead. This all happened because she was a giver, her generous hospitality to the prophet of God allowed her to live in a realm of supernatural activities.

ABRAHAM DINING WITH THE ANGELS

Abraham also was known as the father of faith activated by his long awaiting promise or prophecy that God gave him many years ago. After waiting for few years something happened that gave him an opportunity to activate this pending prophecy. While sitting at the door of his house which was the tent, he lifted his eyes and saw three men approaching from a distance. These three men were total strangers to him and when he saw them he stood up and went to greet them.

And he lift up his eyes and looked, and, lo, three men stood by him: and when he saw them, he ran to meet them from the tent door, and bowed himself toward the ground, And said, My Lord, if now I have found favor in thy sight, pass not away, I pray thee, from thy servant: Let a little water, I pray you, be fetched, and wash your feet, and rest yourselves under the tree: And I will fetch a morsel of bread, and comfort ye your hearts; after that ye shall pass on: for therefore are ye come to your servant. And they said, So do, as thou hast said. And Abraham hastened into the tent unto Sarah, and said, Make ready quickly three measures of fine meal, knead it, and make cakes upon the hearth. (Genesis 18:26)

His response was quite remarkable; it was unusual for a person to embrace strangers in the way he did. When they met he invited them to come and eat a meal revealing his hospitable spirit. The generous spirit in him was revealed. Despite their background or how long he had known them, he welcomed them and shared liberally with them. The Bible has this to say about such a behaviour,

Be not forgetful to entertain strangers: for thereby some have entertained angels unawares. (Hebrews 13:2)

This is a classic portrait of a man who did not know that the people he had invited to enjoy a meal were none other than the angels of the Lord. While they were enjoying his cooking they then announced to him some good news. These news were not new to his ears, he had been told of it be- fore when he had a supernatural encounter with God. It was a reminder of that which he was familiar with, the angels told him he was going to be a father not in the distant future. When his wife, the intended mother of the child, overheard the conversation from the dining table she exploded in laughter. Her laughter I guess was not an arrogant one rather it was maybe some mixed feelings of joy and surprise and disbelief.

And he said, I will certainly return unto thee according to the time of life; and, lo, Sarah thy wife shall have a son. And Sarah heard it in the tent door, which was behind him. Now Abraham and Sarah were old and well stricken in age, and it ceased to be with Sarah after the manner of women. Therefore Sarah laughed within herself, saying, After I am waxed old shall I have pleasure, my lord being old also? (Genesis 18:10-12)

Miracles tend to overwhelm people as the natural man gets overwhelmed when the supernatural occurs. The supernatural power of God can do what is unbelievable, however, the angels noted that his wife laughed.

When she was confronted she denied it. Would it be possible that these angels were not interested in whether she denied laughing or not, rather they were interested in giving her the other part of the message, which was locked up in her laughter? Could it be possible that her laughter would serve as an interpretation and confirmation of the meaning of the child's name? When the child was born he was called 'Isaac', which when interpreted means 'laughter'. It is interesting to note that this supernatural event took place at a dining table. The supernatural was activated by a meal offering. Similarly, this incident also involved a woman that could not give birth, just like the lady in the above-mentioned scenario who also had a problem with child conception. It was through hospitality that a miracle of 'children' was given to them. Another interesting thing is that these two women's sons both had an encounter with death. Scientists call them near death experiences, but these were real death experiences. Upon growing up Isaac was asked by God to be a sacrifice. As he lay on the altar to be sacrificed by his father the Lord spoke.

Typically, he was brought back to life just as the Shunammite woman's son who died and supernaturally rose from the dead. Both their parents were givers. Supernatural giving activates resurrection power. Time does not allow us to share all this power performs, but there are many supernatural works that God did in the lives of those that gave. In the New Testament, we are told about a lady called Tabitha who took care of widows. She did this by knitting for them and giving them warm clothes. One day she died, she was so loved by people that supernaturally God brought her back to life; again, we see another resurrection of a giver.
Then Peter arose and went with them. When he came, they brought him into the upper chamber: and all the widows stood by him weeping, and

shewing the coats and garments which Dorcas made, while she was with them.

But Peter put them all forth, and kneeled down, and prayed; and turning him to the body said, Tabitha, arise. And she opened her eyes: and when she saw Peter, she sat up. (Acts 9:36)

REFLECTION AND PRAYER ACTIVATIONS

1. What is the kind of attitude that must accompany our giving? Every man according as he purposeth in his heart, so let him give; , or of necessity: for God loveth a ____________

2. What does God provide to the sower? For God is the one who_________ for the farmer and then bread to eat. In the same way, he will provide an increase_________and then produce a great_________of generosity in you.

3. Did Abraham pay tithes? And as I may so say, Levi also, who receiveth tithes,___________in Abraham. For he was yet in the loins of his father when Melchisedec met him.

4. The Shunammite woman received a miracle baby through hospitality giving. And he said, Call her. And when he had called her, she stood in the door. And he said, About___________ , according to the time of life, thou shalt .

5.What miracles did the widows giving release? As the story unfolds the meal led the prophet to pray for a miracle that brought _________ into this household. It sustained her and her child throughout the

__________________.

1. 2 Corinthians 9:7 [KJV]
2. 2 Corinthians 9.10 [NLT]
3. Hebrews 7:8-9 [KJV]

4. 1 KINGS 4:13-17 [KJV]
5. 1 Kings 17: 14-15 [KJV]

PRAYER

God give me an attitude of a true giver that does not give grudgingly or murmuring. May I not give sparingly with the understanding that you are giving me much more than I can imagine, help me never to be ungrateful, fill me with the joy of a giver I want to be loved by you as you said you love cheerful givers. You have provided me with seeds may I never go without a harvest. May the generation that comes out of me be a beneficiary of my obedience in my giving just like Abraham was. Make me a hospitable giver like the Shunammite woman. May you multiply my harvest like you did to the widow who gave to the prophet. In the name of Jesus my Lord and Saviour Amen.

CHAPTER 10

SUPERNATURAL UTTERANCE

Preaching is declaring the mind of God. It announces his will and his purposes for his people through the mouth of his preachers. God sent his Son and named him Jesus. He was a preacher who came directly from God. His first preaching took place at the following setting. It was a gathering of people that had come to worship, he stood up and declared the mind of God with the following words that were prophesied years before He came. He did not say something new but confirmed what was already said by God as he went directly into the scriptures and began to expand in the following verse this is what he said

The Spirit of the Lord is upon me because he hath anointed me to preach the gospel to the poor; he hath sent me to heal the brokenhearted, to preach deliverance to the captives, and recovering of sight to the blind, to set at liberty them that are bruised. (Luke 4:18)

He opened His mouth with the announcement that the Spirit of God was upon Him and that the Spirit of God had anointed Him to be a preacher. The preaching of the gospel is a spiritual operation. Preaching cannot be done properly without the inspiration and divine endowment of the Holy Ghost Himself.

The word "preach" according to Webster Dictionary is:
"To proclaim or publish tidings, specifically to proclaim the gospel, to discourse publicly on a religious subject or from a text of scripture, to deliver a sermon."

Preaching is also to give serious advice on moral and religious matters, or, to advise, or, to earnestly recommend. To do all that one must be anointed by the Spirit of God as we saw from the scripture above. The word "anoint" means to have divine enablement, it is to be given the ability to declare the purposes of God through supernatural means. The gospel is the Good News and it reveals Christ, His purpose and destiny, His birth, death, and resurrection, but to decode it properly and preach it, there is a need for supernatural grace. Outside the anointing, people can end up preaching from the spirit of error, which derives out of either, the doctrine of man, or, the doctrine of devils.

Now the Spirit speaketh expressly, that in the latter times some shall depart from the faith, giving heed to seducing spirits, and doctrines of devils (1Timothy 4:1)

Paul forewarned Timothy under the guidance of the Holy Spirit that he must guard against what the Spirit of God was revealing to him. He saw by the Spirit the time was coming that people would depart from the true faith, and pay attention to doctrines of demons. Jesus preached under the anointing of the Holy Spirit, in other words, He was a supernatural preacher. There is a proper way of interpreting the Word of God and it is based on the truth that the Word of God must interpret itself. Jesus' first preaching was from the book of Isaiah, He preached out of an Old Testament scripture. In His preaching, He alluded that the day of the fulfilment of that scripture was now.

If anyone is preaching without the anointing, they may be spreading a spirit of error and heresy. Heresy is part truth, or, it finds its foundation in truth but is not all truth, because to have the truth you must have all the parts put together. When one part of a truth is taken to the extreme, it becomes heresy.

Therefore there must be a proper balance in what is being preached, the Word must interpret the Word.

For precept must be upon precept, precept upon precept; line upon line, line upon line; here a little, and there a little (Isaiah 28:10)

The book of Isaiah is known as the gospel of the Old Testament. It is a book that speaks of redemption; it entails the good news. Preaching must be supernatural and anointed, there are so many categories of preaching, there are man-made preachers, a demon made preacher, religious made preacher, some that are driven by ambition and personalities. There are even churches that are driven by events. It is always important to check the motive behind the preaching.

All scripture is given by inspiration of God and is profitable for doctrine, for reproof, for correction, for instruction in righteousness: (2Timothy 3:16)

Jesus preached from the book of Isaiah, and pointed out to the people that He saw the fulfilment of that prophecy spoken many years ago by the prophet Isaiah. He was not a man-made preacher; He made it clear that it was by the anointing that He was preaching.

The anointing gives divine utterance, the Spirit of God gave Him the ability to decode and download what was in the heart of God. At another place in the scriptures, Jesus began to explain to His disciples who were on their way to Emmaus; they were talking about His crucifixion. He joined them on their way. At first, they did not recognize Him. As they continued to converse with Him, He began to open the scriptures or interpret the scriptures for them. He explained that Jesus was supposed to be crucified, or, to suffer according to the law of Moses, and the prophets that had spoken concerning His destiny. He also mentioned to them that which was written in the Psalms, referring to that which was in the prophets, the law and the Psalms. He showed that all were in agreement concerning His destiny, which included His birth, His death, and His resurrection.

Ought not Christ to have suffered these things, and to enter into his glory? And beginning at Moses and all the prophets, he expounded unto them in all the scriptures the things concerning himself. (Luke 24:26-27)

Some indeed preach Christ even of envy and strife, and some also of good will. (Philippians 1:15)

It is important to guard the attitude behind preaching in order to avoid a spirit of error, and religion. In the Old Testament, the order was that the priests were the custodians of the Word, they were the governmental order of the church. Under the leadership of Moses were Aaron and his four sons, which is a picture of the fivefold ministry revealed as part of the New Testament government order. The apostles, prophets, teachers, pastors, and evangelists in the New Testament were all anointed to serve.

And he gave some, apostles; and some, prophets; and some, evangelists; and some, pastors and teachers (Ephesians 4:11)

He gave some to be what He was to the church, the five-fold ministry gifts as stated above are supernaturally endowed by Jesus who Himself was anointed to preach. He continues to manifest Himself as an apostle, prophet, teacher, evangelist, and pastor through those who are anointed with His anointing. The word of God is supernaturally inspired by God; it takes the same God who inspired the Word to reveal His Word to those that preach from His inspired Word. Preaching is a supernatural declaration under the unction of the Holy Spirit that brings conviction and clarity to the heart of man and causing a desire to change his ways. It produces a conviction to turn from wickedness, to repent and change one's mind and it only comes through supernatural preaching.

Religious ideas and church attendances will never transform the human heart, it takes the supernatural anointed Word of God to penetrate the heart of man as the Word says in the scripture below:

For the word of God is quick, and powerful, and sharper than any two-edged sword, piercing even to the dividing asunder of soul and spirit, and of the joints and marrow, and is a discerner of the thoughts and intents of the heart. (Hebrews 4:12)

The Word of God provides correct doctrinal teachings; it establishes people of God so they are not moved or taken captive by other teachings that do not come from the Word of God. The Word of God is quick, sharp and powerful. Motivational speaking and politics must never a substitute for the word of God. Hence Paul alluded to the fact that he needed prayers so that supernatural utterance may be given to him. The Bible says that we have the mind of Christ.

For who hath known the mind of the Lord, that he may instruct him? But we have the mind of Christ. (1Corinthians 2:16)

Supernatural preaching is communicating the mind of Christ. In the book of Hebrews, we are told to consider Jesus.

Wherefore, holy brethren, partakers of the heavenly calling, consider the Apostle and High Priest of our profession, Christ Jesus (Hebrews 3:1)

It is of paramount importance that in our Christian faith we should put the emphasis on Jesus. All Christian doctrine is founded upon Him. He is the Word and all the scriptures are inspired, or, they are given by inspiration. They form part of what we preach as the doctrine that we ascribe to is founded in the Word of God. It is anointed preaching that brings people into right standing with God. The preaching of the gospel is only foolishness to those that perish, but to those that believe and are in right standing with Him, it balances and empowers their lifestyle.
There are many eloquent speakers, smooth operators, and politicians, however, their word does not transform. It can only amuse people and produce friends and followers, their words do not carry transformation power that can convert hearts. It takes supernatural activity for hearts to be changed.

The writer of the book below says:

How then shall they call on him in whom they have not believed? and how shall they believe in him of whom they have not heard? and how shall they hear without a preacher? (Romans 10:14)

Preachers are sent ones. God appoints and anoints those that speak on behalf of God; unless one is sent he is unable to speak. The speaking of the preachers is a divine utterance; it causes conviction in those that hear. They speak on behalf of God and their message is supernaturally empowered by the Holy Spirit, not everyone must preach. It requires a divine encounter for one to obtain divine revelation to release divine utterance.

Praying always with all prayer and supplication in the Spirit, and watching thereunto with all perseverance and supplication for all saints; And for me, that utterance may be given unto me, that I may open my mouth boldly, to make known the mystery of the gospel. (Ephesians 6:18 – 19)

Paul the Apostle in the above scripture indicated clearly that there is a need for prayer and supplication for all saints and he included himself in the narrative that prayers must be made for him so that utterance may be granted to him. In other words, he knew the difference between his normal utterances and the divine utterance, when one is speaking under the unction of the Holy Spirit he does not speak on his behalf, he is speaking the mind of God into the environment, and that comes only when God is present.

A connection with God reveals the heart of God and causes the speech to be taken over by supernatural utterance so that one gets to speak from the supernatural realm. Jesus preached under the anointing of the Holy Spirit, and when one speaks under the unction of the Holy Spirit it defies human logic, hence Paul says he wanted a granting of the Holy Spirit in his speaking.

The Webster Dictionary defines 'utterance" as follows: Power or a style of speaking.

MY PERSONAL ENCOUNTER OF SUPERNATURAL UTTERANCE

I have my own personal experience when it comes to supernatural utterance. Immediately after my conversion, one day as I was in a place of prayer not many days after I had given my heart to the Lord, I experienced a divine encounter. It all began when I was just hanging out with some friends from the church, I started having an overwhelming feeling that was pulling me with a strong desire to go and pray. I had never felt like that before this was all new to me. As I said I was still new in my walk of faith. The feeling was so strong that I could not afford to ignore it. I had to give in, in short I decided to exclude myself from everyone else and went to a solitary place somewhere in the woods. Upon arriving the sun had almost set however because of this feeling I just needed to pray.

I knelt down and as I began to pray I felt some footsteps drawing closer to where I was as if someone was approaching me. He kept on coming until He was finally where I was. I felt that someone was standing just beside me. Immediately there was an unprecedented overwhelming feeling that words cannot describe that surrounded me. At that point even the tone of my praying changed, my prayer language was supernaturally transformed I spoke languages that I had never heard of from anyone for quite a length of time. They kept on changing and changing, it was an undescribable experience beyond explanation. And the next thing that happened to me I heard the words "raise your head I want to speak to you" I stopped praying for a while, stood up and looked around and there was no one I could see with my natural eyes.

However He continued to speak to me and told me that I was to go to become a preacher of the gospel and He was going to send me to go near and afar, beyond the rivers and beyond the seas. As a young boy at that time this did not make any sense, my economics, my background and a whole lot of things were not substantial for this to amount to anything that I could concur with. I began to question Him and say how is this going to be, I gave excuses, my age was not right, my background was not right. He insisted that, that was going to be my new assignment. This went on for the longest time so much that I lost track of time. It was now late into the night, I then decided to go back.

As I was walking back home He continued to engage me. He gave me an assignment to go to a friend's house which I gladly agreed on. I was keen because I wanted to know whether I had not lost my mind. Upon arriving at my friends place, I delivered the word to him and to my surprise my friend confirmed everything I told him. As if that was all He gave me yet another assignment. There was a bible school in the neighbourhood that He instructed me to go to. Upon arriving I found someone praying. As I opened my mouth to tell this man what I was told word by word everything came to my memory. Again this man was grateful and confirmed that indeed it was God who sent me. To cut the whole story short this was the beginning of my supernatural utterance experience. At some point during that week I was told to go tell my pastor that I was to preach. Again what I was to preach I was given word by word during my time of prayer. My pastor was generous, allowed me to preach on a Wednesday evening service in spite of my inexperience. I had never preached before I knew nothing about preaching. To my astonishment and everyone's astonishment, my friends were amazed at what I was saying, my pastors were all impressed and began to encourage me that indeed God was working through me.

That very night one man stood up and made a public confession that through my preaching he was now going to obey God as he was resisting the calling of God in his life. That night became a turning point for him. I can say my first sermon made someone to go into full time work for the Lord. The following day he went and resigned his day job as a result of my preaching. I recall the words of one of my friends that night who was more experienced than I was. His exact words were "welcome to spiritual administration my friend". I can say this without a shadow of a doubt I have heard God speak through me. I am a strong believer of supernatural utterance where God takes over your speech and grants you clarity of speech and supernatural expressions where people's lives are transformed and miracles take place, including creative miracles through divine utterances. I can confirm that this has been part of my walk of faith I am not kidding. All that God spoke to me that night I have seen it, I have travelled to the nations of the world, beyond the seas beyond the rivers just as I was told by the man that came that night.

One day in Melbourne Australia after preaching as I was praying for people, a lady came for prayer. I opened my mouth and started speaking to her and said to her God was going to prune her like a rose he was going to make her beautiful like a rose. I continued describing the rose, and at some point the Lord said to me "stop and ask her what was her name" to everyone's surprise including myself, her name was Rose. Divine utterance has allowed me to see God speak through me. This lady not only was she Rose she had a condition that God healed supernaturally, little did I know that when she came for prayer God intended to confirm that through the mouth of those that he sends he can release his word to bring blessings, healing and deliverance to those that He loves.

REFLECTION AND PRAYER ACTIVATION

1. What was Jesus anointed to do? The Spirit of the Lord is upon me because he hath_________me to__________ to the poor; he hath sent me to heal the broken hearted, to preach deliverance to the captives, and recovering of sight to the blind, to set at liberty them that are bruised.

2. Why are scriptures profitable? All scripture is given by inspiration of God and is profitable for __________ , for ___________, for instruction in righteousness:

3. How does the word of God establish His people? For the word of__________God is quick, and _________ , and sharper than any two-edged sword, piercing even to the dividing asunder of ___________ , and of the joints and marrow, and is a____________ of the thoughts and intents of the heart.

4. Why does the Bible say we have the mind of Christ? For who hath known the mind of the Lord, that he____________him? But we have the mind of ________________

1. Luke 4:18 [KJV]
2. 2 Timothy 3:16 [KJV]
3. Hebrews 4:12 [KJV]
4. 1 Corinthians 2:16 [KJV]

PRAYER

Lord grant me the ability to preach like Jesus did under the anointing and the power of the Holy Ghost. Grant me the ability not to rely on my own words when I share or speak about your loving grace to those that you want to bring into the kingdom through my words and my actions. May the anointing of the Holy Spirit reveal your love to the lost that they may understand their need for a saviour. May they know the benefits that are found in your word. The instructions for righteousness that are found in your word that is quick, sharp and powerful. That reveals the mind of God, In Jesus name, I pray Amen